The Day Of Pentecost ~., ..., h
The Holy Ghost

Edward Irving

Publishing Statement:

This important reprint was made from an old and scarce book.

Therefore, it may have defects such as missing pages, erroneous pagination, blurred pages, missing text, poor pictures, markings, marginalia and other issues beyond our control.

Because this is such an important and rare work, we believe it is best to reproduce this book regardless of its original condition.

Thank you for your understanding and enjoy this unique book!

THE DAY OF PENTECOST,

OR

THE BAPTISM WITH THE HOLY GHOST.

———

JOHN the Baptist was given to his parents beyond the course of nature, and was filled with the Holy Ghost from his mother's womb, on very purpose to be the forerunner and herald of the Son of God, and to announce his approach and prepare his way, and to declare the great end for which he was sent forth from the bosom of the Father into this sinful and miserable world. Now, if a herald be sent forth to us from a mighty king, we give heed to the word in his mouth, whether it be peace or war, or proclamation of any kind; and seeing that in John is come forth a herald from the Almighty, to announce the arrival of Him upon whom the world's expectations had been suspended from the beginning, and over whom so many promises and prophecies had been pronounced, we ought surely to give most diligent and reverent heed to know that work of God, so mighty and momentous, as that it could be accomplished neither by Moses nor the prophets, by man nor angel, nor creature of what dignity soever, by no one save God's eternal and only-begotten Son. This, then, is the word which God put into the mouth of the man whom he had sanctified from his mother's womb, and separated from amongst the people, to declare in the fulness of time, concerning his dear Son and the work which it pertained to him to perform: " He that sent me to baptize with water, the same said

B

unto me, Upon whom thou shalt see the Spirit descending, and remaining on him, the same is he which baptizeth with the Holy Ghost" (John i. 33). *To baptize with the Holy Ghost*, therefore, whatever that is, is the great thing which Christ is announced to perform. Other things connected with, subservient to, and in preparation for this, he may perform, but this is his noble office, that by which God wisheth him to be distinguished, and which therefore he put into the mouth of his herald. Accordingly we find, that, while other functions are mentioned, this by one and that by another Evangelist, this prerogative of baptizing with the Holy Ghost is the only one which is mentioned by them all. Matthew and Luke add to the baptism with the Holy Ghost these words, "And with fire: whose fan is in his hand, and he will thoroughly purge his floor, and gather his wheat into the garner; but he will burn up the chaff with unquenchable fire" (Matt. iii. 12). Mark hath it simply, "He shall baptize you with the Holy Ghost;" and John adds his sacrifice for the whole world : " Behold the Lamb of God, which taketh away the sin of the world." While, therefore, we give to the atonement and sacrifice which Christ made upon the cross for our sins, "and not for ours only, but for the sins of the whole world," its proper place, as opening the floodgates of mercy that the stream of holiness might pour into the hearts of those who believe ; and while we reserve for him the glory of judging, and consuming in fire unquenchable, all who believe not; we hold up the baptism with the Holy Ghost as his *nobile officium*, his proper and peculiar dignity; and we claim, as the fit style by which he should be announced, " He who baptizeth with the Holy Ghost."

That this is by distinction THE *end* unto which all the other work he wrought, of keeping the law, of condemning sin in the flesh, of openly triumphing over devils in his cross, and over death in his resurrection, were the *means*, is further manifest from the ordinance of baptism which John the forerunner had given unto him as the badge of his commission. He

is the herald of one who is to baptize, and he comes
baptizing: but, that the infinite superiority of Him
that was to come after might be manifested, the
herald baptizeth with water only; he whom he announceth, baptizeth with the Holy Ghost: the one,
the element of nature for cleansing the flesh; the
other, the substance in the Godhead for cleansing
the spirit. Moses had the tabernacle of witness,
which did testify of Christ's flesh, the sacrifice for
sin and the temple of God; Joshua had the host of
Israel, and did testify of Christ the Lord of hosts,
who shall lead his people into the possession of their
everlasting inheritance; David had the kingdom, and
did testify to Christ, who shall sit upon the throne
and rule as King for ever; but John had the sacrament of baptism for the remission of sins, and did
testify of the risen Christ, who should baptize the
church with the Holy Ghost and constitute it His
temple and his abiding-place for ever. The superior
dignity of baptizing with the Holy Ghost, is further
manifest from the superior sanctity of the Holy
Ghost. All manner of blasphemy against the Son
of Man shall be forgiven; but the blasphemy
against the Holy Ghost shall neither be forgiven, in
this world, nor in that which is to come. And why
so? Because the Son of Man is Son of God manifested in the form of mortal life, under the infirmities,
temptations, and disadvantages of this our fallen
estate; but the Holy Ghost is the same Son of God
manifested in the form of that eternal and Divine
life which he entered into by the resurrection from
the dead. The whole work of the Son of Man, until
the resurrection, consisteth in the taking of this
mortal life, and offering it without one sin upon the
cross, to end there for ever; but the work of the Holy
Ghost is not to manifest a mortal life, no, nor even
such a life as Adam was created withal, but that inexhaustible and glorious and eternal life into which
Christ entered at the resurrection, of which he communicated the fellowship to the church on the day
of Pentecost, and which is all the wisdom, all the

knowledge, all the power of God dwelling in the church, and through the church put forth in the deliverance, decoration, government, and blessedness of the world for ever. How much the life of Christ upon the throne of God is fuller, better, and mightier than the life of Adam as he was created, than the life of a poor, oppressed, yet innocent, mortal creature; so much is the manifestation of the Holy Ghost more admirable than the manifestation of the Son of Man, and the sin against the one more terrible than the sin against the other; so much also is the dignity of baptizing with the Holy Ghost a more excellent dignity than any other of all which pertain to Christ: it is his prerogative, his supremacy; which pertains to him as " the beloved Son of God, in whom he is well pleased."

And, though we be not yet arrived at the proper place for shewing forth all the reasons of this paramount excellency, it may be good, for the greater cheerfulness and encouragement of our reader, to give him a glimpse into the glory of the subject here at the outset of our course. The work which fell to the Son of God to do, when he took flesh and blood the same with the brethren, was to redeem it from under the power of sin, by shewing it obedient to the most holy law of God. This having done to the well-pleasing of the Father, the next thing was to render up the life of it as a doomed thing, a thing doomed for having once sinned in Adam; and this was necessary, in order to satisfy the justice of God, which required death for sin; not the death of that person only who had sinned, but the death of that form of being, of that form of life, in what persons soever it may appear. This Christ did: he gave that natural life, which in him had never sinned, an offering unto the justice and holiness of God. And having given it, it was given, and never resumed again; for out of death that form of life which fell into death doth never arise again: it is ended: death is its loathsome and dishonourable inheritance because it sinned. ᵣrection is not Adam's life restored; but another

life, conferred by God, of an infinitely more excellent
kind, in which is contained the fulness of the Godhead in a body. This life, equal in dignity and in
power to the headship, lordship, and sustentation of
all creatures; this life, possessed of capacities equal
to the sitting in God's own throne, and wielding the
sceptre of the world; this life, conscious to the mind
of God, possessed of the energy of God, inhabited by
the light and love and goodness and power of God;
is that which Christ entered into by resurrection, and
communicates to the church by baptism with the
Holy Ghost. He did not come alive again; he was
raised, by the "working of the mighty power of God,
according to the exceeding greatness of his power."
(Eph. i.) That life is of another kind than Adam's
original, or our derived life; it is incomparably more
excellent, more glorious; it is the *ultimatum* of God's
exertion, the perfection and completeness of his
manifestation: he will put forth no more majesty,
he will put forth no more might. Life standeth at
its full-tide mark in Christ: Godhead in him is altogether revealed, confessed, and glorified. Now
this is the possession into which the baptism with
the Holy Ghost introduceth us; this is the fountain
of which we drink; this the power with which we
are anointed; this the life into which we are introduced. Not indeed manifested now in the blaze of
its glory, but under the veil of this corruptible flesh;
yet verily and indeed life of that life, power of that
power, being of that being; "born not of blood, nor
of the will of the flesh, nor of the will of man, but of
God." Take Christ's natural life at its best, it was
but holy mortal life, whose consummation was in
dying a spotless death; a blameless life and spotless
death was its consummation. But of this life into
which he hath entered, and of which we drink in
this baptism with the Holy Ghost, the beginning is
in conquering death; the ending is no where, nor is
the measure yet found; for it "is the fulness of
God," "the stature of Christ." Christ's work in
flesh satisfied God's justice against sin; it paid the

penalty of natural life's transgression; it shewed forth God's holiness in inflicting death upon the world; it opened the way to God for finishing his gracious plans and purposes in the creation of man; it gave him the sinless man, the sin-subduing man, the all-tempted yet all-holy man, upon whom he might confer the full measure of man's intended portion, of God's intended benefits. This Man he could consistently with his holiness reward. In advancing Him, he would be shewn to be not a sin-indulger, but a rewarder of merit. This Man had not turned in his hand like a deceitful bow; this Man had not failed in his trust over the few things of natural life; this Man had not said to his Maker, What doest thou? this Man had not forestalled God's devices; but yielded himself in faithfulness and in confidence, in righteousness and holiness, in patience and long-suffering, to his Creator, to do with him and make of him what he pleased. And, lo! the Creator shines forth resplendent in his goodness by taking him out of the grave, and making him to know the paths of life, and to taste of the pleasures which are at his right hand for evermore. And Christ, having received this new resurrection-life of the Holy Ghost, doth communicate thereof a beginning in the baptism with the Holy Ghost, and intend that the church should be the depositary of it for ever; which she ought to shew forth always, both in this world and in that which is to come: now, by those weak and beggarly instruments of a fallen creature; hereafter by those mighty and glorious ones which shall be put into her hand at the coming of the Lord.

There can be no doubt, therefore, from all these considerations—namely, the official and authoritative announcement of the Baptist, the rite of baptism with which he came attended, the greater guilt of the blasphemy against the Holy Ghost, and the glance which we have taken of the subject itself—that the work with which God doth implicate the dignity of his honourable Son is the baptizing with the Holy Ghost; that if the dignity of Christ as the Son of man standeth in his spotless and all-satisfying sacrifice, his dignity of the Son of God standeth in the prerogative of baptizing with the Holy Ghost: and, if so, no subject can be more precious, if any so precious, to the believer who is the subject of this gracious and glorious work. And if the minister of Christ be his witness unto the world, this, the brightest jewel in his crown, ought not to be forgotten by him; and if he be set for the edification of the church, this, which is the peculiar inheritance of the church, should be continually the theme of his discourse; and if the church be the receiver, the container, and the holder-forth of this excellent treasure, she should be careful to look that she is not hiding it in a napkin, or burying it in the earth. On all these and many other accounts, which will appear in the sequel, I reckon it at all times a most dutiful, and at the present time a most peremptory thing, to set forth in order the mind of the Lord upon this great subject, according to the gift which hath been bestowed upon me by the great Dispenser of the Holy Ghost; to whom I pray, that, for the glory of his own great name as Baptizer with the Holy Ghost, he would not suffer me to fail in this other undertaking for the edifying of his body the church, which is the fulness of Him that filleth all in all.

Now that this high and heavenly office of baptizing with the Holy Ghost was not fulfilled by Christ unto his disciples before the day of Pentecost, is put beyond question by his own express and categorical declaration to this effect after his resurrection, in these words: " And, being assembled together with them, commanded them that they should not depart from Jerusalem, but wait for the promise of the Father, which, saith he, ye have heard of me. For John truly baptized with water; but ye shall be baptized with the Holy Ghost, not many days hence" (Acts i. 4, 5). It is therefore to no purpose to argue that the Holy Ghost had wrought faith in all saints from the beginning of the world; and that the Spirit of Christ was in the Prophets, and spake in

them; and that these very Apostles and disciples had
already gone about putting forth the same powers of
the Holy Ghost as they afterwards did; and that
Jesus, after his resurrection, had breathed on them,
saying, "Receive the Holy Ghost." While these
things are admitted as true, we assert, upon the authority of our Lord in the passage just quoted, that
the great end for which he was announced by John
the Baptist, his proper and peculiar and supreme
office of "baptizing with the Holy Ghost," was not
in any of these gifts and works of the Spirit contained; was something distinct from and far above
and beyond them all; was not accomplished upon
the earth, but sent down from heaven; to perform
which it was expedient, yea, necessary, that he should
go away and be glorified with the Father. And this
is confirmed, if confirmation were needed, by the declaration of John the Evangelist made in these words:
"In the last day, that great day of the feast, Jesus
stood and cried, saying, If any man thirst, let him
come unto me, and drink: he that believeth on me,
as the Scripture hath said, out of his belly shall flow
rivers of living water. But this spake he of the
Spirit, which they that believe on him should receive: for the Holy Ghost was not yet given, because
that Jesus was not yet glorified" (John vii. 37—39).
Now that this thing, which was not done, and could
not be done till after Christ's ascension into the
glory which he had with the Father before the world
was, was actually performed and accomplished on
the day of Pentecost, is manifest from the expression
"not many days hence," that is, ten days after his
ascension. There were fifty days in all between the
Passover, the day of his crucifixion, and Pentecost,
the day of the baptism with the Holy Ghost; of which
fifty, forty were passed with his disciples before his
ascension, "speaking with them of the things pertaining to the kingdom of God." And the work of
the day of Pentecost is further manifested to be the
baptism with the Holy Ghost, both by what took
place, "They were all filled with the Holy Ghost,

and spake with tongues, as the Spirit gave them utterance;" and also by Peter's declaration concerning it, "Having received of the Father the promise of the Holy Ghost, he hath shed forth this which ye now see and hear." And it is further manifest from the power with which they ever afterwards were clothed, and in the strength of which they went about their work of witness-bearing, to which end, among others, the Spirit was promised: "But ye shall receive power after that the Holy Ghost is come upon you: and ye shall be witnesses unto me, both in Jerusalem, and in all Judea, and in Samaria, and unto the uttermost part of the earth" (Acts i. 8). Forasmuch, then, as it is beyond all doubt that the great and chief work of "baptizing with the Holy Ghost," for which Christ came forth from the Father, was on the day of Pentecost accomplished to the church, we ought, in order to understand the subject, carefully to study the record of that day's transactions, whereby that which heretofore had stood in the form of promise and prophecy came to be matter of fact, and gave origin to a new constitution and aspect of the church: and therefore we have given to our discourse the double title of "The Day of Pentecost, or the Baptism with the Holy Ghost."

After these introductory observations, so necessary to the explanation of a subject little treated of in the church, we are prepared to lay down the method proper to this discourse, which is as follows:—That, seeing from the day of John the Baptist this "baptism with the Holy Ghost" began to be prominently presented to the church as the chief object of her desire and expectation, and continued to be so for the seven years which occurred till the day of Pentecost, we ought first to consider the subject in this state, as it lay before the church in the form of promise, variously set forth in the Gospels. Secondly, That, seeing the promise was fulfilled on the day of Pentecost, we ought most carefully to consider the record thereof, with all the passages of Scripture which cast light thereon, that we may have a com-

plete view of the act of fulfilment. And, seeing that
this was to introduce a new era in the church of the
greatest consequence, which no one but God's own
Son in the state of glory was competent to bring in,
we ought, in the third and last place, to consider
this subject of " the baptism of the Holy Ghost "
in the way of its permanent effects, pointing out the
new privileges, powers, and responsibilities which
were thereby brought into and entailed upon the
church. And after this method we will take the
whole subject under consideration : First, The Baptism of the Holy Ghost in the state of promise :
Secondly, The fulfilment thereof on the day of Pentecost : and, Thirdly, The consequences thereof now
and for ever. And again we pray the Father and
the Son, who by the Spirit have brought us thus
far, to carry us prosperously to the end of such a
mighty undertaking.

PART I.

THE BAPTISM OF THE HOLY GHOST IN THE FORM
OF PROMISE.

IT will help us not a little to the right ordering of
this part of our subject, if we shall first notice those
names and descriptions of the heavenly gift by
which Christ drew the desire of his disciples towards
it, during those forty days after his resurrection that
he abode with them on earth before his ascension into
glory. After confirming their doubtful minds, by
shewing them, from Moses and the Prophets, that he
was to suffer and to rise from the dead ; and opening
their understanding that they should understand the
Scriptures—that is, after doing for the whole company of them that office which he had done for the
two disciples on their journey to Emmaus—he said,
" And, behold, I send the promise of my Father upon
you : but tarry ye in the city of Jerusalem, until ye be

endued with power from on high" (Luke xxiv. 49).
That the thing for which they are here commanded
to wait, under the name of " the promise of the
Father," and " power from on high," is the same
with the baptism with the Holy Ghost, is of itself
manifest, and cannot be questioned. But if proof
should be required, it is found in the corresponding
narrative of the first chapter of Acts, where the
" promise of the Father" is identified with " the
baptism with the Holy Ghost " announced by John,
in these words: " and, being assembled together with
them, commanded them that they should not depart
from Jerusalem, but wait for the promise of the Father, which, saith he, ye have heard of me. For
John truly baptized with water; but ye shall be baptized with the Holy Ghost not many days hence"
(Acts i. 4, 5). And with the same heavenly gift is
" the power from on high" identified, in these words
of the same prefatory chapter : " It is not for you to
know the times or the seasons, which the Father hath
put in his own power. But ye shall receive power
after that the Holy Ghost is come upon you : and
ye shall be witnesses unto me, both in Jerusalem and
in all Judea, and in Samaria, and unto the uttermost
part of the earth" (vers. 7, 8). This last passage is
the more to be remarked, as it determines that they
were not qualified for witness-bearing until they had
received those "powers of the world to come." This
work was too weighty for earthly power; for any power
of manhood, of reasonable persuasion, of eloquent
speech, of human wisdom or endurance : it must not
be attempted nor undertaken till the Heavens had
come to the help of mortal man, till the heavenly
life and power of the risen and glorified Jesus had
entered into the members of his body upon the earth.
This establishes the true connection between the two
parts of the corresponding passage of Matthew's
Gospel, with which, like Luke's, it also concludeth:
" And Jesus came, and spake unto them, saying,
All power is given unto me in heaven and in earth.
Go ye therefore and teach all nations, baptizing them,

In the name of the Father, and of the Son, and of the Holy Ghost; teaching them to observe all things whatsoever I have commanded you: and, lo, I am with you alway, even unto the end of the world" (Matt. xxviii. 18—20). If we inquire, further, as to the nature of that power in which they were to go a-preaching, we have some particulars of it given in the corresponding passage of Mark: " And he said unto them, Go ye into all the world, and preach the Gospel to every creature. He that believeth and is baptized shall be saved; but he that believeth not shall be damned. And these signs shall follow them that believe : In my name shall they cast out devils; they shall speak with new tongues; they shall take up serpents; and if they drink any deadly thing, it shall not hurt them; they shall lay hands on the sick, and they shall recover " (Mark xvi. 15—18). These powers of various kinds, into which this is not the place to inquire particularly, were to attend upon the preached word, in order to confirm it; as the same Evangelist immediately declareth, and with the declaration concludeth his Gospel: " So, then, after the Lord had spoken unto them, he was received up into heaven, and sat on the right hand of God: and they went forth, and preached every where, the Lord working with them, and confirming the word with signs following " (vers. 19, 20). From these notices of the Evangelists we observe, that the way in which Christ was wont to speak of the baptism with the Holy Ghost, was, first, as " the promise of the Father, which, *saith he*, ye have heard of me;" and, secondly, as " endowment with heavenly power for the office of bearing witness to his death and resurrection in all nations of the earth, and to every creature under heaven." These two names, " The promise of the Father," and " The gift of power from on high," we ought therefore carefully to note, and diligently to study, as chief heads of this part of our subject; and this we will do, after an observation of the corresponding part of John's narrative, which hath a specialty in it by no means to be passed over.

On the evening of the day he arose from the dead he appeared amongst the disciples, gathered together with closed doors for fear of the Jews, and said, " Peace be unto you;" and shewed them his hands and his feet, to convince them that it was he himself, and not a spirit. And then he said to them again, " Peace be unto you : as my Father hath sent me, even so send I you. And when he had said this, he breathed on them, and saith unto them, Receive ye the Holy Ghost: whose soever sins ye remit, they are remitted unto them; and whose soever sins ye retain, they are retained " (John xx. 21—23). There is no hint in this narrative but that all the disciples were present, the Apostles, the Seventy, and the women ; all, save Thomas, whose absence is specially noted. But as this is a matter of some importance, we think it good to confirm the obvious bearing of the narratives by positive proof from the Gospel by Luke, who recounts the same interview between the risen Redeemer and his fearful flock on the evening of the resurrection day. That it was the day of the resurrection is clear from the perusal of Luke's narra- tive: which contains first the appearance at the se- pulchre to the women; then his appearance " that same day " to the two disciples on their way to Em- maus; then their rising that same hour, and return- ing to Jerusalem, and finding the " eleven gathered together, and *them that were with them;*" and as they were speaking, and recounting what had befallen them by the way, " Jesus himself stood in the midst of them, and said, Peace be with you." And so the narrative proceeds. In a full assembly of his church, Apostles and disciples, both men and women, Jesus spake these words, " As the Father hath sent me, even so send I you ;" and upon the same persons breathed he, and said, " Receive ye the Holy Ghost;" and to the same persons entrusted he the power of remitting and retaining sins. Now the question is, What is this breathing upon them in order to convey the Holy Ghost? That it is not the baptism with the Holy Ghost, we have already shewn from the words

c

of our Lord (Acts i. 4) ; and from the words of this
same Evangelist (John vii. 39). And what then is it?
I think it is the same thing which is expressed by
Luke in these words: "Then opened he their under-
standings, that they might understand the Scriptures"
(xxiv. 45): and in the Book of Acts by these words;
"After that he through the Holy Ghost had given
commandments unto the Apostles whom he had
chosen" (i. 2) : being, as I take it, such an influence
and operation of the Holy Ghost as might enable
them to enter into the instruction which during those
forty days he communicated unto his church. It
was, moreover, a making over to the church, from his
own person, of power to exercise authority, and to
go forth in his name. Moreover, it was the doing by
a sign, and in part, that which was to be perfected
on the day of Pentecost. So far as that inspiration
went, it proved him to be the giver of the Holy
Ghost; it established by a particular instance the
general truth, that the Holy Ghost was breathed
forth from his mouth, and, though the gift of the
Father, was not otherwise than through the Son conveyed to the church. There may be more than this in
it ; more I have not been able to perceive : and as
it doth in no respect stand in the way of our subject,
forasmuch as it certainly is not the baptism with
the Holy Ghost, nor doth in any way supersede it,
perhaps I have spent too much time in endeavouring
to explain it. Only it seemed good not to omit this,
when noticing the other narratives of our Lord's
transactions between his resurrection and ascension
into glory. One thing hath come out of it which is
of great importance, that during those forty days he
transacted with his whole church, and not with the
Apostles only ; that he sent all of them into the
world to witness for him, as he had been sent to
witness for the Father.

With the advantage of these new names, " the
promise of the Father," which they had heard of
Jesus, and "power from on high," to qualify them for
preaching and witness-bearing, we do now return to

open at large the first head of our subject; which is,
"The baptism of the Holy Ghost, as the same is
laid out in promise anterior to the day of Pentecost."
And because the subject of the Holy Ghost's operations are but little understood, I would first discourse
generally thereof, in order to discover that in particular which is termed "baptism with the Holy
Ghost:" and this we will do first *negatively*, by shewing those operations which are distinct from it, and
in the order of time anterior thereto; then *positively*,
what itself is: under which two heads the divers forms
of Divine operations will separately appear, whereof
"baptism with the Holy Ghost" is the third and
most perfect. This done, we shall, in the third and
last section of this Part, exhibit the subject as it
began to be developed from the time when it was
announced by the Baptist, until the time when it
was accomplished on the day of Pentecost.

§ 1. *On the divers Operations of the Holy Ghost, to
separate those which are not " the Baptism with the
Holy Ghost."*

This expression, " the Promise of the Father,"
meaneth not 'which the Father promised,' for it
is added, "which ye heard of me;" but "the promised Father." Christ was the Promiser; and the
promise is contained in the xivth, xvth, and xvith
chapters of John, where he over and over again promiseth to them the possession of and oneness with
the Father, to enable them to do the things which
the Father, dwelling in him, had enabled him to do,
yea, "and greater works than these." All that the
Father hath he promiseth to them in the gift of the
Comforter, and the Father himself, to come unto
them, and to make his abode with them. Christ
promiseth all this " because he was going to the Father," in order to receive it for distribution to his
disciples; and Peter testifies to the fact of all this
being the very gift bestowed on the day of Pentecost:
" Therefore, being by the right hand of God exalted,
and having received of the Father the promise of the

c 2

Holy Ghost, he hath shed forth this, which ye now
see and hear" (Acts ii. 33). But in order to understand the full significancy of what is contained in the
expression " the promise of the Father," it will be
necessary to shew what part of Christ's work in the
flesh was proper to the Son, and what part was
proper to the Father : for every thing which is in
the members must first be seen embodied in the
Head, who is God's model of working, after which we
are predestinated to be conformed. Now, if we can
discover what part in Christ's work was proper to the
Father, that certainly is the thing which is assured
to us in the promise of the Father ; for the Father's
way of working is always the same.

Be it then observed, and borne in mind, that when
the Son became man he never of himself, and by
himself, acted above or beyond the proper limits and
bounds of man's habitation : and whenever he passed
these, whether in the way of knowledge or of power, he
ascribeth it unto his Father ; saying, "The words
which I speak, I speak not of myself," and, "the Father,
which is within me, he doeth the works." To recover
man's possession, and to occupy it in righteousness
and true holiness, is the part of the Son of God when
he hath become the Son of Man : to fill this holy and
obedient Man with a knowledge and with a power far
beyond and above the human or the angelical, or that
of any creature, this is the work of the Father, who
dwelleth in him. The Father took up his abode in
him immediately upon his baptism, coming in the
person of the Holy Ghost in the form of a dove.
Then Christ was baptized with the Holy Ghost; then
he received the promise of the Father; and then also
he was anointed with the Holy Ghost and with power :
and from that time he went forth preaching the Gospel, and " healing all that were oppressed with the
devil, for God was with him." (Acts x.) Anterior to
this he had done the man's perfect part, as the same
is contained in the Law; he had " fulfilled all righteousness, and "well pleased " the Father. And this
he had done, without any indwelling of the Father

speaking, acting temples of God the Father; according as it is written, "And what agreement hath the temple of God with idols? for ye are the temple of the living God; as God hath said, I will dwell in them, and walk in them; and I will be their God, and they shall be my people. Wherefore come out from among them, and be ye separate, saith the Lord, and touch not the unclean thing; and I will receive you, and will be a Father unto you, and ye shall be my sons and daughters, saith the Lord Almighty. Having therefore these promises, dearly beloved, let us cleanse ourselves from all filthiness of the flesh and spirit, perfecting holiness in the fear of God" (2 Cor. vi. 16—18, vii. 1). This operation of the Holy Ghost, to manifest in a believing man the power and presence, the word and work of God the Father, is altogether another and a higher operation than that by which he bringeth us to believe on the Lord Jesus Christ, and enableth us to close with and stand in him. It is the consequence of union, and not the antecedence or the sustenance of it. As the operation of the Holy Ghost brought Christ into manhood, which is generation; so the continuance of that kind of operation brings the elect and believing ones of the Father forth from the bosom of his counsels unto Christ; and this is regeneration, conducted properly under the hand of the Father. Being brought unto Christ, another operation of the Holy Ghost doth wash and cleanse, and feed and nourish us up in him, upon his flesh and blood; and this is under the hand of the Son, being the continuance of that which he put forth upon himself in the days of his flesh, and by which he continually resisted and overcame temptation, and presented himself holy. This Christ worketh in his members continually, and it is properly their life, their nursing, and their feeding, and their fitting to be the temples of God. Then cometh the third and last operation of the Holy Ghost, which is baptism with the Holy Ghost, bringing into the believer, thus united with Christ, the fulness of that inhabitation of the Father which Christ now enjoys for ever. And this is the coming of the Father and the Son to dwell in us, and make their abode with us: this is the thing into which we are searching under the name " promise of the Father," or " baptism with the HolyGhost."

There are, then, two modes of Divine action, two spheres of Holy Ghost manifestation, which are distinct from the baptism with the Holy Ghost, which have been in being and operation since the beginning of the world, and are by Christ redeemed from sin and death. The first is the work of creation, purely of God, without any helping hand of the creature, which was nothing. And when the creature became dead through sin, it was in a more helpless, hopeless state, even than when it was nothing; being now in a state of active enmity against God, all the powers he had given to it actively turned against him ; dead to good, active to all evil. To bring it out of this state, therefore, requireth no less, but a greater, energy of God than to create it out of nothing at first. This energy was put forth in the generation of the Son, holy, and pure, and lively unto good, out of the sinfulness and deadness of corruption ; and it is continued in the church in the regeneration of the wicked by the power of God through the word. This, which is the act of election, the drawing of the Father, without which no one can come to Christ, is a purely Divine work, with no help, but all hindrance, from the creature. And this is the first operation of the Spirit, viz. in overcoming the rebel will of the creature, and leading it unto Christ, whom by nature it hates with all its heart ; and this work of the Godhead, which begins in regeneration, is never ceased from by the Father, but constitutes the basis of a continual love, looking for, and longing after Jesus.—The second operation of Godhead is done, not without, but through the creature whom he hath made. When he had brought man out of nothing, and given him to occupy a certain room in creation, to fill a habitation, and to exercise a power, and that no mean one, he did not intend that he should therein act all independent of his Maker, but that he should acknowledge unto him his whole being, and by a

dependent faith and willing obedience receive a
continual supply of the Holy Ghost, to nourish and
sustain the same, and fit him for all the will of his
Creator. This is the second manifestation of Godhead power in the creation, which we see in the infinite forms of life all around us,—in the flowers of the
field, in the endless functions of animated nature, and,
above all, in the infinite thoughts and purposes of
the mind. This is what is expressed continually in
the Scriptures when descanting on the creation as the
work of the Spirit of God; and Paul applies it as
the standing argument of a God, " In that he gave
them fruitful seasons;" and as the ground of our responsibility, " For in him we live and move and have
our being" (Acts xvii. 23). The course of nature
and the course of thought are still a manifestation
of the Holy Spirit, although bedimmed and belied
by the work of the devil and of wicked men. It is
because they do not *choose* to retain God in their remembrance, that God " gave them up to a reprobate
mind." Now this second form of the Spirit's operation having been by sin transformed, Christ came to
redeem; and, putting himself into the case of man, he
gave heed unto the Spirit of the Creator, and presented his creature always good and well-pleasing in his
sight. He lived by faith; he hoped when he was on
his mother's breasts; he did nothing by himself or
of himself, but depended upon God, as ever helpless
new-born babe did upon the mother and the father
who were the authors of its being. The eternal Son
in the bosom of the Father, willing to glorify his
Father by shewing his sufficient provision for the
creature, and that it had fallen through no defect
of God's care, did submit to be brought into the
case of the creature, and found himself by the Spirit
in the virgin's womb; and exercising ever the same
meek resignation, even when girt about with infinite
foes, and hoping even upon his mother's breasts, he
did ever receive that operation of Godhead which
was laid up in store for the creature man, but which
no man as yet had received, only because no man
would exercise the trust in God necessary to receive

to constitute a man a convert to Christ; yea, and a converter of others. I know not whether there be a contrast intended between " the way of the Lord " and " the way of God " in this passage : if so, it would still more remarkably sustain our doctrine, that the baptism with the Holy Ghost is *the way of God's dwelling and working in us.* Wherein John's baptism came short, is fully narrated in the following verses, where Paul asks the Ephesian disciples, " Have ye received the Holy Ghost since ye believed ?" And they answered, " We have not so much as heard whether there be any Holy Ghost." [This translation carries error in the face of it, for John's baptism announced a Holy Ghost, and Jesus as the dispenser thereof: it ought to be, " whether the Holy Ghost be yet."] " Then said Paul, John verily baptized with the baptism of repentance, saying unto the people, That they should believe on him which should come after him, that is, on Christ Jesus. When they had heard this, they were baptized in the name of the Lord Jesus. And when Paul had laid his hands upon them, the Holy Ghost came on them ; and they spake with tongues, and prophesied " (Acts xix. 4—6). John's baptism, therefore, went the length of repentance, change of heart, or regeneration ; and remission of sins, or cleansing by the blood of Christ from our sins, through vital union with him by faith. It took in both the doctrine of being born again, which the Lord preached to Nicodemus (John iii.) as of the earthly things, seen in all the washings and purifications of the Law, and in the baptism of John, the re-union and consolidation of all these into one solemn ordinance ; and also the doctrine of feeding upon his flesh and blood, which he preached in the synagogue of Capernaum as shewn forth in the manna, and in all the sacrifices (John vi.) ; but it contained not " the heavenly things," which he could not enter upon with Nicodemus (John iii. 12), nor yet to the men of Capernaum, as he announced in almost the self-same words: compare John iii. 13, with vi. 62 : in both of which

passages he refereth to his ascension into his pristine
glory as preceding the ministry of the heavenly
things : wherefore also they are called "heavenly,"
because they came down from the heavenly floor, and
hold of the heavenly state about to be upon the earth
in the age to come ; wherefore also they are called
(Heb. vi. 2) " the heavenly gift," and the " powers of
the world to come."

These remarks are of the utmost importance, not
only as confirming and entirely establishing the doctrine as to what the baptism of the Holy Ghost *is not*,
but also for an end of charity, which, though I have
kept it out of view, lest it should warp the reader's
judgment, I have had fully in my mind—namely, for
preventing the church from falling into despair upon
the discovery that she possesseth not the baptism
with the Holy Ghost, whose standing sign, if we
err not, is the speaking with tongues. For though
our guilt be great in having foregone this our inheritance, and lost those gifts which are without repentance or withdrawal on the part of God ; and
though our loss in all ways be inestimably great,
and God's glory obscured, and Christ's love not exhibited, and the church's union all dismembered, and
the world defeated of her proper witness, all through
our unfaithfulness ; yet is it comfortable to know that
we and our fathers may still have been Christians, true
members of Christ, washed from our sins in his blood,
and changed of heart, notwithstanding we have no
signs of the Holy Ghost's baptism, nor tokens of an
indwelling Father, to produce. And this I believe to
be the exact condition into which the church hath
fallen back since the first three centuries ; the same
as the condition in which the church stood anterior to
the day of Pentecost, with a Baptism for repentance
and remission of sins, with a Lord's Supper for union
to Christ and feeding on his flesh and blood ;—in
which the Ephesian church was anterior to the visit
of Paul, " speaking and teaching diligently the things
of the Lord....mightily convincing the Jews, and shewing out of the Scriptures that Jesus is the Christ ;"

yet without the baptism with the Holy Ghost, which
it is Christ's chief office to bestow, the church's chief
glory to possess, the Father's great desire to exhibit
in the sight of the world. But some will say, If we
have regeneration and union with Christ, we are well
off; what more would we have? Brother, have what
it pleaseth Christ to give thee. Art thou going to
stint the Father and the Son? Art thou going to do-
mineer over their givings? God forbid! Art thou to
say, I will take what is needful to save me, but any
the least work for God's glory I will not do; I will
not charge myself with any of his affairs, but I will
burden him with all mine? Oh, brother! this baptism with the Holy Ghost, which I am about to teach
thee of, is the very glory of God in the sight of angels
and of men: wilt thou not be the bearer of it? Whilst
thou heard not of it, thou couldst not desire it; but
now that I am about to teach it thee, I beseech
thee to open thine ears, for it is the most glorious
and blessed theme of which I have ever yet discours-
ed, or of which thou hast ever yet heard. Come
not over the course of our sweet communion with
such fallacious questions as these, ' But what then
are we to make of our fathers, who knew little or
nothing of this, and had no marks of possessing it;
nor the Reformers; nor the saints and martyrs later
than the third century?' I have given thee rest on
this question. They might still have regeneration
and remission, and the grace of both sacraments:
but God is leading us of this age back to fountains
of which our fathers never drank; which were open
to them indeed, as to the first Christians, but the way
unto them was not known. Neither say unto me,
' And what art thou, who presumest to pass beyond
the Luthers and the Calvins?' I am a minister
of Christ, as well as they; one as near to God as
they; to whom his book is as free as to them; and
I seek to occupy the work of my day and generation,
as they also did. Let us not trouble ourselves with
such irrelevant matters, but proceed, Book in hand,
and the Spirit of truth in our heart, to open what

the baptism with the Holy Ghost is, having opened
already what it is not.

§ 2. *The same subject continued, with the view of
defining precisely what the Baptism with the Holy
Ghost is.*

Having shewn that the baptism with the Holy
Ghost is neither regeneration, nor yet union with Christ
to be partakers of his flesh and blood ; neither the
work of the Father to draw us to Christ, nor yet the
work of Christ to impart unto us holy manhood; we
now come to examine what it is. And the answer
is very simple : " All beyond the created powers and
faculties of man, which man hath ever possessed,
doth now possess, or shall possess for ever." There
are only these two things, the creature and the Creator ; the one having its bounds and limits within the
sphere of creation, the other having His place and
habitation above and beyond it : not of creation a
part, though the Author and Sustainer of its being ;
not mixed up with it in any way, nor inhabiting any
part of it; but out of the world : " I came forth from
the Father, and am come into the world : again, I
leave the world, and go to the Father" (John xvi. 28).
Of these creatures it hath pleased the Father to
choose one for a dwelling-place, which is man ; and
for this end he made man in his own image, and after
his own likeness ; a fit house for such an Inhabitant.
It is the greatest act of grace on the part of God,
to choose such a shrine from out of which to shew
himself; and thrice blessed and honoured is the
creature of whom he maketh choice. In choosing
man for a habitation to walk in, and abide in, and
shew himself out of, God doth not mean to make
himself a man, nor yet to make man God, nor in any
way to mingle the Creator and the creature; but by
the organs and faculties of that creature to put forth
his own surpassing beauty, supreme majesty, infinite
love, and almighty strength. To obtain for the Father
his great and gracious end, of which he had been
long defeated by the sinfulness of man, his own Son

became man, and accomplished to be sinless; and so became the habitation of the Father's fulness, the brightness of his glory, and the express image of his person : " It pleased (the Father) that in him all fulness should dwell—all fulness of the Godhead in a body." In the man Christ, always man, and at no time more than man (for whatever is more than man to ascribe unto Christ, is to bereave the Father's work in the man Christ, who is the Son of God become man), the Father dwelt, and did things such as never man did. He knew what never man knew, " for in him dwelt all the treasures of wisdom and knowledge." He spake as never man spake : " The Spirit of the Lord did rest upon him, the spirit of wisdom and understanding, the spirit of counsel and might, the spirit of knowledge, and of the fear of the Lord" (Isai. xi. 2). He overcame the devil and all his angels, and cast them forth; he healed all manner of diseases by the word of his power; he commanded the winds and the waves, and all the elements, by the same free word. He created bread; he made men, and animals, and fishes of the sea, to serve him; he raised the dead; he abolished death and the grave; he apprehended all God's mind, and he uttered it, failing nothing; he shewed all God's love and long-suffering and patience; he preached God's Gospel : " The Spirit of the Lord is upon me, because he hath anointed me to preach the Gospel to the poor; he hath sent me to heal the broken-hearted, to preach deliverance to the captives, and recovering of sight to the blind, to set at liberty them that are bruised, to preach the acceptable year of the Lord " (Luke iv. 18, 19). These are all Divine works; works proper to the Creator, and to no creature. Christ, as a creature, was a poor weak mortal; a worm, and no man. This he consented to be; this he was, in the form of a slave; but what power was given him! what liberty! what Godhead wisdom! what Godhead virtue! Truly might the Baptist say, " For he whom God hath sent speaketh the words of God : for God giveth not the Spirit by measure unto him. The Father loveth the Son, and hath given all things into his hand " (John iii. 34, 35) : and well might Christ himself say, " All things are delivered to me of my Father : and no man knoweth who the Son is, but the Father ; and who the Father is, but the Son, and he to whom the Son will reveal him " (Luke x. 22) ; and again, " Believest thou not that I am in the Father, and the Father in me ? The words that I speak unto you I speak not of myself : but the Father, that dwelleth in me, he doeth the works. Believe me that I am in the Father, and the Father in me : or else believe me for the very works' sake " (John xiv. 10, 11). The works did testify that God was with him, because they were works proper to the Creator. The works of Christ were as truly Godhead works, as the works recorded in the first chapter of Genesis. But it may be asked, ' How could this be, seeing creation hath not been added to ?' The answer is, That though creation hath not been added to, it had all come into a state of activity against God ; which to withstand and turn again, is a proof of an antagonist power greater than creation, that is, the power of the Creator. All creation had fallen into a state of death, which to revive again into life argued a power equal to, yea, and greater than, the power of bringing them all out of nothing. To do these things was not man's province, himself mortal, nor Adam's at first, nor angel's, nor any creature's, but only God's ; and so God exhibited himself in action, through the powers and faculties of the Man Jesus. He revealed the Father in will, in thought, in word, in act. To do this, was in his case the baptism with the Holy Ghost. And what is it in ours ? The same, the very same. ' And are we to expect the same things to be displayed in us ?' Yea, and greater things than these. ' Explain this more perfectly.' That I will, brother, if God permit.

To ask the question, ' Whether any thing which was done in Christ is to be expected by his members ?' is to betray great ignorance of the way of God. What was done in Christ, was done in him as man ; he became man in order that it might be

done in him. For this end He, who was the Creator
of all things, became the creature man, that in the
creature man he might receive those things which
had been intended for man from the time of his creation, yea, before the world was made. These purposes concerning man were not made for any other
being but for man; and Christ, in order that they
might be realized, became man. That his Father's
infinite grace, predetermined upon this much-favoured
creature, might no more be hindered or postponed,
Christ himself took that creature's form, and presented the faultless subject for the Father to do all his
will upon. And the same honours which Christ hath
attained as man, are reserved for every man who walk-
eth in his footsteps; and there is a certain portion
who are elected in Christ to the fellowship of all his
glory, and shall not by any means be suffered to miss
of it; of whom he could say, before he left the
earth, "The glory which thou gavest me I have
given them; that they may be one, even as we are
one" (John xvii. 22). To make a question, therefore,
whether what Christ in his manhood attained to in
the world, be not the privilege and property of other
men as well as he, is not to understand the doctrine
of the incarnation at all. I say, *in the world,* because
that honour which he hath with the Father out of
the world, sitting on his throne, we may not aspire
to; but "as he is, so are we in this world" (1 John
iv. 17). In the days of his flesh he shared with men
his powers against unclean spirits and diseases:
"Behold, I give you power to tread on serpents and
scorpions, and over all the power of the enemy: and
nothing shall by any means hurt you. Notwithstanding, in this rejoice not, that the spirits are subject unto you; but rather rejoice because your names
are written in heaven" (Luke x. 19, 20). And not
only so, but he communicated to them of that anointing of the Holy Ghost which he had received for the
preaching of the Gospel, when he sent them forth,
and covered them with the fearful sanction thereof:
"And whosoever shall speak a word against the Son

of Man, it shall be forgiven him: but unto him that
blasphemeth against the Holy Ghost, it shall not be
forgiven. And when they bring you unto the synagogues, and unto magistrates and powers, take ye no
thought how or what thing ye shall answer, or what
ye shall say: for the Holy Ghost shall teach you in
the same hour what ye ought to say" (Luke xii.
10—12). And he could say of them, in his inter-
cessory prayer, "I have given unto them the words
which thou gavest me; and they have received them,
and have known surely that I came out from thee,
and they have believed that thou didst send me"
(John xvii. 8). This liberal distribution of that, his
flesh-inheritance of the Holy Ghost, to those who believed on him, ought to be the surest guarantee of his
power and his purpose to do the same with that
larger store which he should receive when he ascended
unto his Father: and Peter expressly declareth,
that the thing which was seen and heard on the day
of Pentecost was nothing else than this very communication unto his members of what he himself
had come to the inheritance of: "This Jesus hath
God raised up, whereof we all are witnesses. Therefore, being by the right hand of God exalted, and
having received of the Father the promise of the
Holy Ghost, he hath shed forth this, which ye now
see and hear" (Acts ii. 32, 33). Now the Lord was
not slow to assure his disciples of that mindfulness
which he would have of them when he should ascend
to his Father, and of the Father's own love to them:
" For the Father himself loveth you, because ye have
loved me, and have believed that I came out from
God" (John xvi. 27). The supply of supernatural
power and providence which he bestowed upon his
disciples during the days of his flesh, to fit and furnish
them for being his heralds in the cities of Israel, was,
as I have said, cut short when that hour and power of
darkness came on, to which he looked forward with so
much apprehension, and all but prayed that it might
not befal him. Then, as it seems to me, the Father's
blessed presence and sweet influences were hidden from

his soul, and he was left to struggle in naked manhood
with all manhood's enemies; until, after having en-
dured the whole of man's bitter portion for transgression, the Spirit of the Lord came mightily upon
him in the separate state, and he burst the gates
of hell, and rifled the house of corruption, and entered
triumphantly into the ways of eternal life. During
this period of suspended power within himself, there
was also a suspension of it with his disciples. The
Shepherd being smitten, the sheep were scattered
abroad. But when he returned from his perilous
voyage back again to his well-beloved little flock,
that very night he breathed on them, and they received the Holy Ghost; thereby proving to them that
he was again in full possession of power. But he
told them, as we have seen, that a few days must
elapse before he would fulfil all he had promised
to them, because he was "not yet ascended to his
Father and to their Father, to his God and to their
God." For in the days of his flesh he always made
the gift of the Holy Ghost to depend upon his going
to his Father: as for example, "Verily, verily, I say
unto you, He that believeth on me, the works that
I do shall he do also; and greater works than these
shall he do, because I go unto my Father" (John xiv. 12).
The reason is, that the gift might be known to be
neither of the man, human; nor of the earth, earthly;
but of the heavens, heavenly; of the Father, divine.
The earthly things are what God gave into man's
hand to rule over and enjoy: the heavenly things are
what belong not to man in natural or creation right;
but what belong to God in his proper sphere, to man
only as the favourite creature of God, made to be his
habitation of delights and his seat of power. That
the Holy Ghost, when given by Christ, might therefore be known to be from the Father, it was necessary that Christ should first go to the Father and
receive it, and from thence dispense it to the church.
No doubt Christ entered into a fulness of the Holy
Ghost upon his resurrection, whereof the gift at his
baptism was but to him the first-fruits, as the baptism

of the Holy Ghost given to us now is but the first-
fruits of that full harvest which at our resurrection
we shall enter into. With all the oneness which he
then enjoyed with the Father, he was still in humiliation, a man of sorrows and acquainted with grief,
open at every pore to temptation, and exposed to
every assault of the devil, needing the ministry and
consolation and strengthening of angelic spirits; but
when he ascended into glory, behold, the mightiness
of the Spirit is such as words can hardly express,
and the dignity and power of life, into which it bore
his once mortal members, is far above the level of
every creature, into the very throne of God : and being thus exalted, endowed, and possessed, he is given
to be the Head over all to the church, from which no
elevation, as no adversity, can divide him; " neither
height nor depth :" and this church is his body,
into which he ever poureth all the strength of the
Head, so as that she becomes " the fulness of Him
who filleth all in all " (Eph. i. 23). In his exaltation we are exalted : " we are risen with him, and
seated with him in the heavenly places ;" " we are
made partakers of all spiritual blessings in the heavenly places in Christ." In one word, the whole tenor
of Scripture representeth his church on earth to be as
truly one with him in the copartnery of his celestial estate even now, as she is one with him in the
fellowship of his sufferings. His disciples in the
days of his flesh received share of the powers then
possessed by him; and when he received new powers,
" the gift of the Holy Ghost," on his ascension to
the Father, they received on the day of Pentecost
the full share thereof, to the extent of this body's
power to contain, and of this world's power to bear
the sight and the hearing of them. There is as perfect sympathy between Christ in glory and his members on the earth, as between the head and the members of the body, between the trunk and the branches
of the vine; and therefore we are not only to expect
that the works which he did we shall do also, but
that greater works we shall do, because he is gone to

the Father, and hath received power which in this world he did not possess.

Are we, then, to understand by the baptism of the Holy Ghost and the indwelling of the Father, that in us the works of God are to be manifested as they were manifested in Christ? Yes, we are so to understand. And is the life of Christ an ensample to the believer in its miraculous and divine works, as it is to him in its humility, meekness, and holiness? Even so. And may we really hope to enjoy what he enjoyed of the Father's sweet and gracious in-dwelling? Hear his own words, in that blessed discourse concerning the promise of the Father: " These things have I spoken unto you, that my joy might remain in you, and that your joy might be full" (John xv. 11). And may the believer expect that very peace which the holy and harmless Jesus enjoyed always, through his oneness with the Father? Hear his own words: " Peace I leave with you, my peace I give unto you: not as the world giveth, give I unto you. Let not your heart be troubled, neither let it be afraid" (xiv. 27). And may we expect the same insight into the mind of the Father, which he had? Hear his own words: " But the Comforter, which is the Holy Ghost, whom the Father will send in my name, he shall teach you all things, and bring all things to your remembrance, whatsoever I have said unto you" (xiv. 26). And may we expect to have the same power of withstanding the world's snares, and rebuking its hypocrisy and sin? Hear his own words: " But when the Comforter is come, whom I will send unto you from the Father, even the Spirit of truth, which proceedeth from the Father, he shall testify of me: and ye also shall bear witness, because ye have been with me from the beginning" (xv. 26, 27). But did he not say that he did the works which none other man did? May we expect to do these? Hear his own words, so oft quoted: " Verily, verily, I say unto you, He that believeth on me, the works that I do shall he do also; and greater works than these shall he do; because I go unto my Father" (xiv. 12). And, to

E

take a particular instance, when the disciples marvelled to see how soon the fig-tree which he had cursed was withered, " Jesus answered and said unto them, Verily I say unto you, If ye have faith, and doubt not, ye shall not only do this which is done to the fig-tree, but also, if ye shall say unto this mountain, Be thou removed, and be thou cast into the sea, it shall be done" (Matt. xxi. 21). And in both these instances, to make assurance doubly sure, he gave to the believer a *carte blanche* of power, to be filled up according to his own mind : " And all things whatsoever ye shall ask in prayer, believing, ye shall receive " (ver. 22). But may we expect the same fulness of knowledge which he possessed ? Hear his own words : " Howbeit, when he, the Spirit of truth, is come, he will guide you into all truth : for he shall not speak of himself; but whatsoever he shall hear, that shall he speak : and he will shew you things to come. He shall glorify me: for he shall receive of mine, and shall shew it unto you " (John xvi. 13, 14). And, to shew us that there is not any thing which Christ hath received of the Father that the same Comforter will not bring into us, he addeth, " All things that the Father hath are mine: therefore said I, that he shall take of mine, and shall shew it unto you " (ver. 15). And, in confirmation of this promise by the fact, read 1 Cor. ii. 7 ; and 1 John ii. 20, 27 ; and Eph. iii. 19 ; iv. 13, 15 ; and innumerable passages of the Epistles, which, because they come not within the scope of this part of our subject, we only refer to. And we might refer to hundreds of passages in the Epistles, and indeed to the whole New Testament, written after the day of Pentecost, wherein our community of power and working with Christ, and our possession of the indwelling Father, are every where taken for granted and presupposed, as the basis and being of the church, rather than enumerated as one of her properties. But one passage I must quote, in confirmation of all which hath been declared : " Now there are diversities of gifts, but the same Spirit: and there are differences of

administrations, but the same Lord: and there are
diversities of operations, but it is the same God which
worketh all in all. But the manifestation of the
Spirit is given to every man to profit withal. For to
one is given, by the Spirit, the word of wisdom; to
another, the word of knowledge, by the same Spirit;
to another, faith, by the same Spirit; to another, the
gifts of healing, by the same Spirit; to another, the
working of miracles; to another, prophecy; to another, discerning of spirits; to another, divers kinds
of tongues; to another, the interpretation of tongues:
but all these worketh that one and the self-same
Spirit, dividing to every man severally as he will"
(1 Cor. xii. 4—11). This is the description of the
manifested Holy Ghost, of the inworkings of the
Father, of the endowments of Christ to the several
members of his church. It is not now the place to
go into the detail of these gifts, but the bare enumeration we give, as amply demonstrative of the great
truth which we are opening, namely, *That the bap-*
tism of the Holy Ghost doth bring to every believer
the presence of the Father and the power of the Holy
Ghost, according to that measure, at the least, in which
Christ during the days of his flesh possessed the same.

My idea, therefore, concerning the baptism of the
Holy Ghost, or the promise of the Father, is simply
this, That it is a superhuman supernatural power, or
set of powers, which God did from the beginning
purpose to place in man, but which he accomplished
not to do until his own Son had become man, and
kept man's original trust. He had not the perfection
or pre-eminence because he was God, but because
he was the first man who had kept man's charge. It
had entered into the purpose of God from the beginning, to make man the seat of his own Divine power,
and through him to reveal his working for ever in the
midst of the created universe. The superhuman, the
" divine nature," was intended from the beginning for
man; but God could never get it rightly and fitly
bestowed upon him, because he failed in his hand,
and kept not his first estate. He was not faithful over

the few things of nature, but brought himself into
sin and death; and how shall God recompense such
a one with any blessing, and be not himself partaker
with him of his sin? How God should gain his end of
bringing the superhuman and divine into man after
he had become a sinner, so as not himself to be a
sin-indulger, this was the great difficulty and ob-
struction, which Christ removed out of the way, by
perfecting holiness in our nature, cursed, corruptible
and mortal though it had become. Then God attained that for which he had longed, and accomplished
his great purpose of making man possessor of " all
power in heaven and in earth." And, forasmuch as
this superhuman and infrangable life, this " life of
God," was intended for mankind; for the unity of
the brotherhood, and not for any single man, or set
of men; Christ, having received it, doth straightway
proceed to dispense it unto others, and commands it
to be proclaimed as the privilege of " every creature
under heaven." Who are they who are quickened
together with him, raised together with him, and together with him seated in the heavenly places? Those
who were dead in trespasses and sins (Eph. ii. 4—7).
The superhuman and divine powers resident in the
risen Christ, are as much the birthright of every man,
through the riches of the mercy and the love of God,
as disease, death, and dissolution are, through his
justice and his holiness; the purchase of the one
being the righteousness of the man Christ, the purchase of the other being the sin of the man Adam.
That this superhuman endowment of power divine
was originally within the range of man's capacities,
yea, and desires, is, we have already observed, manifest from the way in which Satan shaped his
temptation; " Ye shall be as gods:" for to make any
thing a temptation, there must be a natural adapta-
tion of the subject to the object. The same was manifest also in the creation of man " in God's image
and likeness." Wherefore? That God might shew
himself through the same. Not that man might be
seen to be God, but that God might dwell in, and be

seen dwelling in, man. It reduces you at once to anthropomorphism, if you do not recognise the truth that God was to be seen dwelling in the image, not the image as the representative of God. An image the representative of God, is the essence of idolatry: God dwelling in that form of creature which is made to be his image, is revelation or manifestation of himself. In the very creation of man, therefore, I see the purpose of inhabitation, and endowment with attributes divine, as clearly contained, as I see it fully accomplished in the resurrection of Christ. And when man fell, I see the same truth contained in the promise, that " the Seed of the woman should bruise the head of the serpent." But I see it more brightly in the cherubim, in which God dwelt from thenceforth. For what is the cherubim, but the symbol of the church gathered from amongst men ; as they themselves declare (Rev. v. 9), and as we have demonstrated at large in our Lectures on the Revelations. Now, from this cherubim the mighty power of God ever proceeded ; as at Sinai, in the wilderness, in Canaan, and every where ; both the word of wisdom and of knowledge, and all the Divine acts of power and judgment. All which proceeding from the cherubim, declares the truth, that in man it was the purpose of God at length to deposit power superhuman and divine. The same thing is taught in all the Prophets ; to whom it was given by the Spirit to foresee and foretell the future, which is a divine faculty ; also to controul and counteract the course of wickedness, disease, and death, and to do acts superhuman and divine—as making the sun and moon to stand still, cleaving the flood, and performing all wonderful works. Any one, the least of all these miracles, done by man, is proof to me that man is intended for having and holding the administration of manifested Divine power. For there are no exceptions or anomalies with God ; no appearances, or occasional actings : every thing is on a system, and to an end, into which every incident and particular worketh most harmoniously. All the wonders done in the person of what are called angels—as at Sodom, before Gideon, Manoah, and others—were done by the Angel of the Covenant, which is Messiah, which is the Son of God, within the bounds and limits of resurrection manhood. In the carrying into effect of these miraculous powers, I well believe those angels or invisible spirits do serve, but always under the superior direction and guidance of man, who is the proper and immediate shrine of God for word and work divine. All these apparitions, promises, types, and symbols of God dwelling in man, were realized fully in the ascension of Christ into glory. The resurrection life, is life of God within the man; it was first consummated in Christ, and belongs to us in virtue of union with him. We have it not in full, nor can have, till the resurrection. We have it only as a baptism till then; as he had it as a baptism from the day of his baptism until the day of his agony. Then, I think, it was withdrawn; and with what augmentation of all our troubles the withdrawal of it is attended, was evidenced in the awful horrors of that dreadful interval called " the hour and the power of darkness." It was withdrawn then, that he might finish the work in naked manhood, which in naked manhood he had begun. He kept the law without any baptism of the Holy Ghost; and thus also he contended with the powers of wicked men, and angels of hell and death: after finishing the former part, he received the baptism of the Holy Ghost; after the completion of the whole, he received the fulness of the Holy Ghost. And so we, sealing first into John's baptism of repentance and remission of sin, by believing on Christ, the Lamb of God that taketh away the sin of the world, do receive the baptism of the Holy Ghost; and when we have finished our course, by overcoming death and the grave, we shall share in the fulness of Christ's present power and government of all things. We shall be made partakers of the Divine nature, when we have escaped the pollution that is in the world through lust (2 Pet. i. 4). And through eternity, God, residing in his church, shall therein administer all government, and work all blessedness for his creatures. And by the church shall be manifested to angels and principalities, in the ages to come, the manifold wisdom of God; and the church shall be the image in which God shall be seen; a perfect transparency, hiding none of his glory, and yet always having the felicity of rendering it intelligible and operative of all good. Blessed distinction, to which thou hast lifted us up, O glorious Son of God, by becoming humbled and lowly Son of Man!

And now we are able to see the full force of the name, " Promise of the Father," which is given to the baptism of the Holy Ghost. The Father, as distinguished from the Son after the incarnation, is the same with God, as distinguished from man; because the Son ever acteth as man, and brought himself into the dependence of a creature, in order to shew forth the Godhead of the Father, who doth sustain, strengthen, and glorify him. The promise of the Father, is therefore essentially the promise of Godhead power. The promise of Messiah, which had been put into the mouth of all the former prophets, is the promise of God in the form of man, or the promise of the Son of Man to come and redeem man, and man's habitation, from the power of evil. And when Messiah comes, the Prophet of prophets, his mouth also is filled with a promise. He comes not only to be the end and seal of all former prophecies, but to originate a far higher and more glorious promise than they had brought; which is, the promise of the Father. They promised the Son; the Son, when he comes, promised the Father. They promise manhood's Redeemer; he promiseth manhood's Glorifier. They promise holiness in flesh, and life from the dead, through the incarnation of God; he promiseth Divine wisdom, power, and glory, through inhabitation and inworking of God. Therefore he could properly say, " The promise of the Father, *which ye have heard of* ME."—of *him*, and not of any *former prophet*—for though the former prophets had given

hints of the day of Pentecost, yet did they not speak
of it as the inhabitation of the Father; "For no one
knoweth the Father, but the Son, and he to whom
the Son shall reveal him." The promise of the Father,
is the promise of God to dwell in them, and act in
them, in what ways are proper to God; that is, in
ways above the ways of man, or angel, or any creature. If it be more particularly inquired, in what
way? I answer, in all those ways in which Christ
wrought after his baptism; every one of whose works
was a manifestation of the Father; a true Godhead
work, which no one but God is able to perform. The
working of God is seen in creation, in the things which
were done during the first six days. Christ's miracles were akin to them. He gave life, when he healed
the man with the withered hand; he created matter,
when he made the five loaves to feed five thousand,
and to fill twelve baskets with their fragments: he
gave words to the elements, and his word was a law
unto them: he commanded the spirits, and they
obeyed him. These works are works proper only to
God; and in all of them he did glorify the Father,
by protesting that he did them not of himself, but
by the Father who dwelt in him. Besides these, he
manifested the Father in a way which had not been
done in creation. For in creation there was no sin
present, and the Father's bearing towards sin could
not therein be revealed. His severity against it was
manifested by the disease, death, and dissolution of
the things which he had made; but further than
this there was no distinct revelation till Christ came,
at least none in action, or only such as to foreshew
what was then to be accomplished. The Father in
Christ healing all manner of diseases, and casting
out all manner of unclean spirits, did most remarkably shew the finger of God, and accomplish all the
words written in the Old Testament concerning his
power and office as the healer of diseases; and,
finally, the resurrection of Christ, which he devoutly
ascribeth to the Father (Ps. xvi.), doth shew him as
the destroyer of sin and death, and the expeller of

them from creation. Now the promise of the Father, which Christ gave to all who should believe upon him, is no less than the promise of a power of God in them to do all these works of God in the sight of an evil and rebellious and gainsaying world, that they may be left without all excuse in saying that there is no God, or that God is not good and gracious. The church is intended to be the witness, yea, the image of God; and God through the church intendeth to reveal himself to the sight and blessedness of every creature.

This also is the reason why the baptism of the Holy Ghost is called " power from on high," or power from heaven, where God dwells. Not *power* merely, but *power from on high*. There is a power which is given to men, the power proper to us as creatures within our own habitation of the earth,—power to rule the animal creation, power to know and take care of the things which spring out of the earth. This belongs to us as creatures; we received it as our talent, to improve for the Master's use, and for our own advancement, if we should be found faithful. Being found faithless, we forfeited it; and there remained nothing but a fearful looking for of judgment and fiery indignation to consume us. In this state the Son of Man found the family whom he had loved before the foundation of the world; and having set himself to the work, he recovered to us our original estate, and with it our original power; power in the will over the members of the body, over the world, and over the temptations of the devil. This we receive in Baptism and the Lord's Supper; the one for regeneration, the other for crucifixion of the flesh, and empowering of the members thereof unto all holiness. But all this, being received, is but earthly power. Power from on high is power of God, to whom the rule and government of the heavens appertaineth. He gave the earth unto the sons of men, but the heavens he reserved unto himself; and power in that region we can only possess by possessing God. For that which distinguisheth God from his creatures

is this, that he only ruleth in the heavens. This he
hath not delegated, nor will delegate. He holdeth
it in his own hands; nor can it be possessed, save by
possessing him: and when he comes, he brings it
with him. Therefore Christ could not bestow this
power until he had ascended into the heavens, and
received all power in heaven as well as in earth. And
inasmuch as Christ enjoyeth both these regions of
power, to dispense them to whom he will, he is proved
to be both perfect God and perfect man: and inasmuch
as we come to him in order to receive them at his
hand, we acknowledge him to be both perfect God
and perfect man; and no one who will not seal to
this confession, can be partakers of either sphere of
power. And thus, by beginning in lowly manhood,
Christ attaineth unto perfect Godhead; and we, by
sharing with him of his holy manhood in the sacrament of the Lord's Supper, do attain unto the inheritance of his divine and heavenly power. And
therefore the Christian calling is called a heavenly
calling; not to heaven merely as a place, but to the
functions and offices of that place, which are altogether divine. Therefore also we are said to be " blessed
with all spiritual blessings in the heavenly things "
[not *places* only, but *things* also, and chiefly, as it is
translated in the discourse with Nicodemus, John iii.]
Therefore it is also called " the heavenly gift," and
" the powers of the world to come;" that is, the
powers which in the world to come shall rule and
preside over the creation; and which are at present
hid with Christ in God, except so much of them as
is revealed in the church, for an earnest of the inheritance of power which we shall afterwards receive.
Of these " heavenly things " our Lord would not
discourse to Nicodemus, because he was not yet
acquainted with the " earthly things," which were
exhibited under his eye. But after the day of Pentecost brought them amongst us, they ought to have
been a chief part of the discourse of the church; and
for not being so prized, they have fallen out of our
hand: but, now that they are found again, like the

Book of the Law in Josiah's time, we do well to
make great account of them, and to set forth the
whole subject in order, as we are labouring, by the
help of God, to do.

Having thus opened the doctrine, both as to what
the baptism with the Holy Ghost is not, and as to
what it is, we ought now to confirm the same from
the Gospels in a more formal manner than we have
yet done; but first we will gather into one paragraph
the sum of what hath been set forth in these two
sections. There are three Persons in the blessed
Trinity, the Father, the Son, and the Holy Ghost; or,
to take the names used by Christ, God the Father, the
Son of Man, and the Comforter. Jesus, being about
to leave the world and go to the Father, made this
remarkable promise unto all who should believe on
him : " He that hath my commandments, and keepeth them, he it is that loveth me : and he that loveth
me shall be loved of my Father; and I will love him,
and will manifest myself to him. Judas saith unto
him (not Iscariot), Lord, how is it that thou wilt manifest thyself unto us, and not unto the world ? Jesus
answered and said unto him, If a man love me, he
will keep my words ; and my Father will love him,
and we will come unto him, and make our abode
with him. He that loveth me not, keepeth not my
sayings : and the word which ye hear is not mine,
but the Father's which sent me " (John xiv. 21—24).
Here is a promise that the Father and the Son should
come unto every living believer, and stay with him.
Now, nothing is more certain than that the Father
and the Son are both out of the world ; and how
then should they be able to abide in the believer?
By sending forth the Holy Ghost, whose office it is
to bear the united and yet distinct substance of the
Father and the Son wherever he goes, and make them
to be felt in their heavenly influences wherever he
abides. It is the Father and the Son coming and
dwelling in us in the substance of the person of the
Holy Ghost. And so the presence of the Comforter

in the church is the presence of the Father, and the presence of the glorified Son of Man. He supplies us with the fellowship of their harmonious mind : as it is written, " And truly our fellowship is with the Father, and with his Son Jesus Christ." Though, therefore, the work which we are searching into be properly done under the hand of the Comforter, which is the Holy Ghost, it is verily and truly a work of communicating to the believer both the Father and Son; the inworking of God the Father, and the fellowship of the power and glory of Christ our risen Head. It is so, as hath been said, with all the works of God. The Father originates the purpose in his own will, and ever works in it as the originating and presiding will : as it is written, " Work out your own salvation with fear and trembling : for it is God which worketh in you both to will and to do of his good pleasure " (Phil. ii. 12, 13) ; and again, " One God and Father of all, who is above all, and through all, and in you all " (Eph. iv. 6). Then cometh the Son, who is the Word to declare the purpose, and the person to fulfil it, and give it real outward living form. Now, the purpose of the Father being to exhibit his power and glory in the creature form of man, the Son did therefore become man, and work out every feature of the Father's glorious purpose; and then he sitteth on the throne of the Father, the living image of the invisible Father. And to him we must all be conformed : " That he might be the first-born among many brethren;" " that in all things he might have the pre-eminence [might be the first, might first it]. To do this, to work in us the image of Christ, which is the image of God, is the part of the Comforter, or the Holy Ghost : what the Father hath willed, what the Son hath informed, it is the part of the Holy Ghost to carry into effect in the creature. When, therefore, Christ had attained to the completeness of the Father's purpose; when he had reached the ultimate and perfected form of human nature, and was the fulness of the Godhead embodied in life, appearance, and action ; the time was come for the Holy

Ghost to undertake his part in the glorious work, and to bring the Father's elect up to this standard form of being. And not till now could the Spirit undertake this work; because not till now was the work finished and perfected in the person of the Son. Just as in creation the purpose of the Father must first be realized in the Son, by his taking to himself the form of Word or Wisdom—not of flesh or body, but of word or wisdom—before the Holy Ghost could proceed to bring the creatures out of nothing; having respect therein to the perfect image of the purpose seen, or rather heard, in the Word (for the Holy Ghost worketh nothing after his own mind, but always after a model or plan which is seen in the Son): so in this work of advancing, decorating, and glorifying the creature which God had made, he may not come forth until he hath the model after which to work, in the perfected, glorified Son. And when the Comforter comes, what else is it to do but to bring us into the very same form of creature subsistence into which Jesus, after his perilous and sorrowful voyage, hath at length attained? What is it, then, that the Comforter doth, but to bring Christ into us, to make us to be as Christ is? And because Christ came to his present glory only through the inhabitation and in-working and outshining of the Father, the Comforter must bring both the Father and the Son to dwell in us: the Son as the informing word, the feeding flesh, the holy life; the Father as the Godhead power, working in us God's will, informing us with God's mind, actuating us with his purposes, enabling us with his might, and filling us with his fulness. The work is done under the hand of the Comforter, or the Holy Ghost; and being done, is the manifestation of the Holy Ghost, which to blaspheme is to commit the unpardonable sin: and the work which the Comforter doth, is to bring the Father and the Son to dwell in us; and therefore it is called the promise of the Father, and the glorifying of Christ.

There are, therefore, three spheres of Divine operation in man, to every one of which the Father and the

Son and the Holy Ghost co-operate, and over each one of which one of the three Persons presides respectively; so as that, in bringing man to perfection, not only the unity of the Three Persons in one substance, but also their distinctness of personality in the same, should be shewn gloriously forth. The first sphere is creation, the second is incarnation, the third is inhabitation: the former under the hand of the Father, with the co-operation of the other two Persons according to their offices; the second under the hand of the Son, with the same co-operation; the other under the hand of the Holy Ghost, with the same co-operation. Creation under the hand of the Father begins at the beginning of things, and proceeds until the creature be brought to the Son, and joined to him by living faith. And this work exhibits the Father, his origination of all, Himself only self-originated : this is shewn forth in his originating the creatures out of nothing : next his holiness, in visiting the sins of his creatures with punishment; and his right over them, in visiting them with death, which is the suspension and cessation of their life and being in that form in which it was given : next his love to them, even in their most abject state; his quickening them when dead in trespasses and sins, his raising them together with Christ, and seating them along with him in the heavenly places. This, the creation, sustentation, and right over the life of his creatures; this his punishment of them by death for sin, and his reward of them with new and infrangible life for righteousness; hath been continually shewing forth in man since his creation, is shewn forth in every man who comes to Christ, and was perfectly epitomized in Christ, who gave himself into the Father's hand, to be generated of him a frail man, and to be treated as the vilest of men, and to be put to death for the sin of men, and to be raised again to eternal, immortal, and infrangible life. In this work the Son and the Holy Ghost co-operate, but in a subordination to the Father : the former as the Word which created, which smote the sinful creation, which

revived it with promise again, and which buildeth a
sanctuary of flesh whereinto flesh might flee and
be safe : the latter as the Breath of Life, to come and
to go, to animate and to conform, to bring forth and
to produce, to change and to forsake, and otherwise
to substantiate in creature the Word of God, which is
not creature, but intermediate between God and creature. But while the Son as word, and the Spirit as
substance of the word, do their offices unto creation,
mortification, and regeneration of the creature, they
do it in subordination of the Father, under whose
hand the work thus proceedeth, from its origin in
nothing, aye and until our union with Christ, the
new head of creation.

The second work, which proceedeth under the hand
of Christ, the Son of Man glorified, is the work of
washing the creature from all its sins, informing it
with perfect righteousness, and making it to stand up
again before its Maker, and, though mortal, to do its
Maker's good will, and enjoy his good pleasure, and
be well-pleasing in his sight, keep his law, and shew
forth the image of his holiness. This work, wherein
Christ is made unto us righteousness, wisdom from
God, sanctification, and redemption, is a work done
unto every believer, from what time he is drawn unto
Christ and given unto him by the Father, and from
that time for ever. Nor doth this supersede the
former work of creation, but redeems it from sin unto
goodness, from Satan unto God ; adding nothing to
it, subtracting nothing from it, but establishing the
ends of creation, in defiance and despite of all evil
spirits and evil men. I say, this work of redemption is
from the beginning to the ending of it under the hand
of the Son ; and the Father and the Holy Spirit act
subordinately ; the former ever leading the creature
unto the Healer that he may be healed, effectually
resisting the antipathy which is in our members unto
Christ through sin, and inducing us to make our
case known to him. But there the Father stops : he
doth only bring the lame, diseased creature to the door
of the Physician ; this service of love he doth, and

no more: to Christ belongs the service of healing, and binding up, and beautifying, and strengthening the man for all manly purposes of communing with God and serving him. And the subordinate part of the Holy Ghost, in this work of redemption, is to go between the Physician and the disabled creature, and to carry into exact operation and effect the Physician's most wholesome and sure remedies. Because, in point of fact, the Physician is out of the world, and the patient is in the world ; and who can bridge that chasm but a Divine Person, who may both fill the infinite of Godhead and contract himself into the region of manhood, and continually intervene between these two ? Also, because the remedy is applied in the spirit of man, and not in his flesh, which can be constrained, but not cured ; its poison continually counteracted, its enmity covered and masked, and its rebelliousness enforced, by the vigorous life and health infused into the spirit from the risen Christ, which the Holy Spirit continually supplieth.

Now, the third work, which I have named inhabitation, and which is the proper subject of this discourse, being what is called the " baptism of the Holy Ghost," " the promise of the Father," and the gift of " power from on high," is superinduced upon the two other, but neither stints nor supersedes them. They go on beneath ; the mighty hand of the Father sustaining the nothingness of the creature's being; the mighty hand of the Son redeeming the sinfulness of it ; and now the mighty hand of the Holy Ghost comes in to fill it with Divine attributes of wisdom and knowledge and power. The Father gives the materials, the Son frames them into a living temple, the Holy Ghost fills them with the glory of God. This work of the Comforter is the most wonderful of all. That what came out of and in itself is nothing should be capable of producing the various sensations, emotions, and affections of human life, is wonderful : that what is become mortal, pressed down on all sides with the law of sin and dissolution, should be recovered, against itself, to bring forth the fruits of holy living, is still

more wonderful: but that it should be made capable
of receiving and sustaining the life of God, of having his mind, and of working his works, is a thing
which passeth understanding, being in very deed the
mighty power of God. The great account which is
made of the resurrection of Christ, in all the Scriptures, as " the exceeding greatness of God's mighty
working " (Eph. i.), and of the baptism of the Holy
Ghost, which is the first-fruits thereof—called " the
power from on high," as if nothing else were worthy
of that name—do prove how much more vast is this
than every other manifestation of Godhead unto men.
To make this erroneous mind of ours capable of discerning truth infallibly, to make this trembling and
stammering lip capable of uttering words before
which death and the grave and the devil stand dis-
covered and dismantled, to make this fearful heart
capable of confidence in the face of all ungodly con-
federations, and this palsied hand to strengthen with
all the power of God—these are things which far sur-
pass the speculation, and almost the belief, of man.
And had we not seen it accomplished in the feeble-
ness of Jesus Christ, who calleth himself " a worm,
and no man," we should not have believed it possible
to be done in mortal man : and had we not the assurance of Him who is the Truth, that the like works,
and greater, were to be done in them who believe, we
should have thought it a very wonderful thing, done
once, upon an extraordinary occasion, for an extraordinary end, by one who was an extraordinary person,
God as well as man, and never to be renewed again :
but having his word and the facts of all the Apostoli-
cal history for it, we believe, as we have written, that
this is the third and highest sphere of God's operation in man, carried on under the hand of the Holy
Ghost, whose part it is to bring both the Father and
the Son, or the Son indwelt by the Father, the life
of glorified manhood, into all the members of the
body, that is, into all who believe.

One word further, before concluding this inquiry
into the divers operations of the Holy Ghost. These

three spheres, over which each several Person of the
Godhead presideth, with the other two subordinated
to him, are not disjointed, but pass the one into the
other, and prepare the one for the other—the creation
for the regeneration, and the regeneration for the
glorification ;—and every man, in having the Gospel
preached to him, hath them all and altogether preached to him. Yet are they capable of subsisting apart,
and are found subsisting apart ; and, being so found,
bring each their several responsibilities. The unevan-
gelized part of mankind is responsible to the Creator
for his gifts of creation and providence ; the evange-
lized part is responsible for the faith of the Gospel,
and regeneration, which is the fruit thereof; but the
baptized part is responsible for the fulness of the
Holy Ghost, as conferred on the day of Pentecost.
These parts are, by name, the Heathen, the Jew, and
the Christian : the first, capable of the sin against
the Father; the second, of the sin against the Son ;
and the third, of the sin against the Holy Ghost;
and if now the Christian church should refuse the
gifts of the Holy Ghost, again proffered to her, the
end will be irremediable destruction. Moreover, as it
is the Father who possesseth the first region, and
presideth over it ; so is it his to pass any one out of
it into the second, whither no one can come otherwise than by the giving of the Father : the bride of
the Lamb must be given away to him by the Father.
Even so no one can be passed into the third region
of the Holy Ghost, out of the second region of the
Son of Man, but by the authority and act of the
Son of Man. And this is the reason why it pertains
to him to baptize with the Holy Ghost. His act of
baptizing with the Holy Ghost is, like the Father's
act of regeneration, a transference out of one state into
another. But as in regeneration the Father useth the
Son, the incorruptible Seed; so in passing into the spiritual state the Son useth the Holy Ghost, the Spirit
of power: and as ever, after the former act, we are under
the hand of the Son, to be by him led and guided ; so
ever, after the latter act, we are under the hand of the

Holy Ghost, to be by him used for the glory of the
Father and the Son.

And let this suffice for teaching what the baptism
with the Holy Ghost is. It is an act of Christ's,
whereby he doth give to his church the Holy Ghost,
to dwell in them, and to work in them all the joy and
consolation, all the word and power, which reside in
himself; to the end that, in obeying the motions of
the Holy Ghost within us, we may shew forth in the
world, and to the world, the goodness of God, and
the power and glory of the Son of Man, who sitteth
in God's throne, and exerciseth all the power of the
Father in his presence.

§ 3. *The further confirmation and exposition of the
doctrine set forth above concerning the Baptism of
the Holy Ghost, from the Scriptures of the Old
Testament, and from the Gospels, where it is contained in the form of promise.*

In the categorical and explicit declaration of the
doctrine of the baptism with the Holy Ghost given
above, both as to what it is and what it is not, having been guided entirely by the word of God, especially by the Lord's promise in the Gospels, we may
be thought to have anticipated the matter of this
section altogether: and, indeed, in as far as the right
definition of any subject, and the enumeration of
any proposition, doth contain in its bosom the demonstration and all the details thereof, we may be
said to have anticipated, in the two former sections,
not only the substance of that on which we now
enter, but also of this whole discourse ; and we
might, without further addition, dismiss it as it now
stands, seeing all that follows is only the develop-
ment, illustration, and confirmation of the doctrine
now delivered. Nevertheless, because the doctrine
is very precious, and almost entirely neglected, we
count it good to adhere strictly to our method as laid
down above, though it should carry us into a wider
range than we thought of at first; the more, as what
remains must consist chiefly, or almost entirely, of

Scripture proofs and illustrations, taken first from the Old Testament, and secondly from the Gospels.

I. John the Baptist, in announcing this great operation of baptism with the Holy Ghost as about to be done under the hand of Jesus of Nazareth, which is the Lamb of God that taketh away the sin of the world, doth give no reference to the Old Testament, so as to direct us to any places where the subject is there hinted at, or directly prophesied of. This was reserved for Peter, against the day of Pentecost, who citeth a prophecy of Joel to this effect (Acts ii. 16); as Paul also doth a prophecy in the book of Psalms (Eph. iv. 8); and another from the book of Isaiah the prophet (1 Cor. xiv. 21); and another from the book of the Law (2 Cor. vi. 16—18). But though John himself doth not, upon the occasion of our Lord's baptism, refer to any Scriptures of the Old Testament concerning this matter, our Lord himself doth so, in two instances: the one, when he entered on his public ministry in the synagogue of Nazareth (Luke iv. 16—22); the other, when he lifted up his voice aloud in the temple on the last and great day of the feast of tabernacles (John vii. 37—39). The former appeals to the lxist chapter of Isaiah, as containing the prophecy of his own baptism with the Holy Ghost; and the latter refers to some part or parts of Scripture, where it is said of him that believeth, "out of his belly shall flow rivers of living water," as containing the promise of the Holy Ghost, which was given after he had ascended into glory. Now, because this head of discourse is devoted to the promises or prophecies of the baptism with the Holy Ghost, and all these are by the inspired interpreters declared to be such, we must now, however briefly, examine and consider each of them: and this we shall do in the order of their delivery, beginning with that contained in the Law.

1. The Apostle, in one of the topics of his Second Epistle to the Corinthians, being minded to dissuade them from uniting themselves with unbelievers in any permanent relation, lest they should be drawn

aside from that course of perfect holiness to which
he urgeth them forward, doth seek to accomplish this
end by many considerations, of which the principal
one is contained in these words : " And what agreement hath the temple of God with idols ? for ye are
the temple of the living God ; as God hath said, I
will dwell in them, and walk in them ; and I will be
their God, and they shall be my people. Wherefore
come out from among them, and be ye separate,
saith the Lord, and touch not the unclean thing ;
and I will receive you, and will be a Father unto you,
and ye shall be my sons and daughters, saith the
Lord Almighty" (2 Cor. vi. 16—18). And the same
doctrine of holiness enforceth he by the same consideration of being members of Christ, in whom God
dwelleth, and, who in our unity with Christ, constitute
the temple of the Holy Ghost, 1 Cor. vi. 13—23 (compare with Eph. ii. 19—22, and 1 Pet. ii. 4, 5). The
reason, however, for which we quote it here, is because
it makes reference to a passage in the Old Testament,
as containing the prophecy and promise of God's inhabitation of his people. The passage cited by the
Apostle is as follows : " And I will set my tabernacle
among you : and my soul shall not abhor you : and
I will walk among you, and will be your God, and
ye shall be my people" (Lev. xxvi. 11, 12). The
same truths are more fully developed in Exod. xxxix.
43—46. In both passages the tabernacle, "sanctified by my glory," is the presence chamber of God
amongst them ; and God declareth that he hath
" brought them forth out of the land of Egypt" for
this very end, " that he might dwell among them."
Now the Apostle declareth, in those passages of his
Epistles just referred to, and in many more, that we
are that temple ; and Christ, after his baptism with
the Holy Ghost, declareth the same of himself (John
ii. 21) : he the foundation and chief-corner stone,
we the stones builded thereon and bound together
thereby. Not openly, but covertly, not in naked
presence, but in the habitation of a temple, doth God
propose to dwell and walk amongst his people ; and

not directly, but by Aaron and his son, to hold communication with them, as their Oracle and King. This enclosure (περιποιησις), within the boards and curtains of which God dwells in his glory, and from the secrecies of which he gives forth his decrees, and which is conscious to his blessed indwelling, the Apostle, in the passage before us, teacheth us to consider as a figure of those who have received the Holy Ghost, the promise of the Father. The tabernacle in the midst of the children of Israel is the symbol of the church in the midst of the world,—a portion of men whom the Lord hath chosen for himself, and in whom he is pleased to dwell, forth of them to speak, and thence to make his terrible and dreadful acts of power and judgment to be felt. Now, to my mind, the church regenerate by the grace of baptism, and edified into manhood by the grace of the Lord's Supper—or, in other words, anointed with the life and mind and Spirit of Christ Jesus—is the temple or tabernacle without its glory; and the baptism of the Holy Ghost is the glory coming thereinto, in the concentration of all that power and terror which clothed Sinai; of all that holiness and judgment which spake the Ten Commandments from thence; of all that graciousness and mercy which communed with Moses, and forbare so often with the stiff-necked people. All which ever came forth of the pillar of cloud by day, of the pillar of fire by night, from the morning of the overthrow of Pharaoh till the time of its departure in Ezekiel's days, is conveyed into the church by the baptism with the Holy Ghost, and hath resided in her since the day of Pentecost, and shall yet come forth of her before her period be accomplished. This will still more clearly appear when we shall have considered the next promise of Scripture concerning this supernatural baptism.

2. The Apostle, in his Epistle to the Ephesians, first teacheth, that Christ, ascended into supreme and unrivalled glory, and clothed upon with all power in heaven and earth, is so exalted and endowed for our sakes who believe on him, that we may be partakers

in full of his power (i. 19); of his resurrection life
(ii. 5, 6); his heavenly seat and blessedness (i. 3);
yea, and all the fulness of God (i. 23); even as the
body partaketh the life, strength, wisdom, and glory
of the head : then sheweth he how Gentiles as well as
Jews were brought into the unity of this body of
Christ, through the putting away of all sin by the
blood of his cross; and did all together, with and in
the Head, constitute a holy temple, in which God
might dwell and receive worship for ever (ii. 13—22):
and he afterwards proceedeth (iv. 3) to enforce for-
bearance and love by the sevenfold bonds of unity in
which we are joined, as the one body, by the one
Spirit of Christ. And because the variously gifted
persons, Apostles, prophets, evangelists, pastors,
teachers, &c. were apt to become puffed up in their
gifts, and envious one of another—yea, and the occasions of party and schism in the churches, one saying,
" I am of Paul," and " I of Apollos"— he explaineth
how they were all but gifts bestowed by Christ after
his ascension upon his church, as the appointed means
of perfecting the saints in holiness, of manifesting the
word and Spirit, and of edifying the body of Christ
up to the stature of perfection ; as he expresseth it
in another place: " Who then is Paul, and who is
Apollos, but ministers by whom ye believed, even as
the Lord gave to every man ?" (I Cor. iii. 5). In the
bosom of this argument concerning Christian unity, the
Apostle introduceth a reference to the lxviiith Psalm,
as containing the prophecy of the gifts of the Spirit
poured out from Christ, when from the lower parts
of the earth he had ascended into the highest heavens,
even into the very throne of God. The passage is
as follows : " Thou hast ascended on high, thou hast
led captivity captive : thou hast received gifts for
men ; yea, for the rebellious also, that the Lord God
might dwell among them " (ver. 18). The person is
Jesus Christ the man [for " for men," is, literally, " in
the man "]; the subject is the bestowal of the gifts
of the Holy Ghost by the glorified Man upon his
disciples, both the household of the saints and the

rebellious Gentiles ; the end is, that they might be
builded together into a holy temple, or tabernacle, for
a dwelling-place of the Most High, wherein he might
be seen and served, from whence might go forth the
word of his power, and unto which the footsteps of
all creatures might reverently come and worship. To
construct such a living temple, Jesus, after having
ascended on high, receiveth the Holy Ghost, and
therewith endoweth certain persons master-builders,
builders, and office-bearers of every name, to work in
the work, until " it groweth unto a holy temple in
the Lord " (Eph. ii. 20). The grand type of which
was given in the man Moses, who was a witness in his
house of the things which Jesus was to accomplish.
After Moses had delivered the captivity out of Pharaoh's hand, as Jesus did his church out of death
and him that had the power of death, he did ascend
up unto Sinai—"gat him up unto God"—which an-
swereth to the ascension of Jesus into the glory of
heaven. And what doth he there? He there receiveth
the plan of a tabernacle for God to dwell in ; which
having well considered and faithfully imprinted in
his mind, he doth proceed to build it by means of men
whom God endowed with gifts of the Spirit for that
very end. And when builded, God doth come into
it with his glory, and resteth there amongst the
people, giving oracles and executing justice and judgment in the midst of them. This work, of building
men as living stones into a spiritual temple, Christ
hath been going on with ever since the day of Pentecost, by distributions of the Spirit to certain men,
Apostles, prophets, and others, who should, by spiritual teaching, discipline, and rule, be continually
rearing up the glorious walls of gold, silver, and precious stones, all fire-proof, which shall nobly abide
the day that shall burn like an oven and consume
all the hay and wood and stubble which unwise and
unholy builders have builded thereunto. And when
this holy habitation, " the tabernacle of God," the
new Jerusalem, is completed, then shall come to pass
what is written by the Prophet Haggai, and by the

Apostle Paul (Heb. x. 37) spoken of as still future
in his days : " Yet once, it is a little while, and I will
shake the heavens, and the earth, and the sea, and
the dry land ; and I will shake all nations; and the
Desire of all nations shall come : and I will fill this
house with glory, saith the Lord of hosts" (Hag. ii.
6, 7). This now is the view of the baptism of the
Holy Ghost as given in the lxviiith Psalm, That
Christ, the great builder of the temple, did thereby
endow and commission his servants, in their several
ranks and orders, to go about the work of labouring
with him, and under him, in preparing men, and ad-
justing them to their several places in that living
temple, the church, which the living God shall live
in for ever. And if it be asked, How men are fitted
to such a high and holy vocation as that of holding
and containing the manifested and communicable fulness of God ; the answer is, By being endowed with
the same Spirit which the builders are endowed
withal. For in this temple the stones as well as the
builders are "lively," or alive, and the builders are
themselves no more than foundation stones : " Built
upon the foundation of the Apostles and the Prophets." In what way, therefore, those master-
builders, the Apostles, were fitted to be precious and
strong foundations, are the others fitted to be stones
in that house not made with hands; even by a measure, each according to his place, of that gift of the
Spirit which was poured out at Pentecost.—And
what is my office as a minister ? To minister the
Spirit unto the hearers.—'What saidst thou ? to
minister the Spirit ?' Yea, brother.—'The *word*, surely
thou meanest?' I mean what I say, brother; even
this, That to minister the Spirit is the calling of the
minister of Christ; and I tell thee, that he who
thinketh to minister the word without the Spirit,
thinketh to slay men and not to save them. What,
knowest thou not this? read the iiid chapter of the
Second Corinthians, and thou wilt find that these
words are all synonymous,—" ministers of the New
Testament," "ministers of the Spirit," " ministra-

G

tion of the Spirit," "ministration of righteousness;"
and that this, and this only, is "the ministry which
we have received." Haply thou thoughtest that the
name "minister," by which my office is denominated,
meant a servant of men: thou erredst: it meaneth
a servant of the Lord Jesus Christ, for the purpose
of serving out to his members that manifold power
of the Holy Ghost whereof He is the storehouse, and
which he now is bestowing upon all who believe, in
order that they may glorify the Father in speaking
his word and doing his works, such as Christ did,
yea, and greater too. Dost thou say, ' But thou art
a bold man?' I answer, Yet no more than a faithful
one; and at thy peril be less, whoever thou art.

3. The third instance in which we can with authority say that the subject of the baptism with the
Holy Ghost occurs in the form of promise, is that of
the Prophet Joel, which Peter expressly declareth
was fulfilled on the day of Pentecost (Acts ii. 16),
when "the promise of the Father," and "the power
from on high," fell upon the church. The passage
in Joel stands remarkably wedged in between the
two parts of his prophecy; all before it concerning
the destinies of the Jews, all after it concerning the
destinies of the Gentiles. The Jewish burden having been fully closed, as it usually is, with assurances
of perfect and perpetual blessedness, the prophet
thus discloses the purpose of God in respect to the
outpouring of the Spirit upon "all flesh," as well
Jew as Gentile; which began in the Jew on the
day of Pentecost, and went on spreading abroad to
all nations along with the preaching of the everlasting Gospel, and after a long silence hath again been
revived amongst us: "And it shall come to pass
afterward, that I will pour out my Spirit upon all
flesh; and your sons and your daughters shall prophesy, your old men shall dream dreams, your young
men shall see visions: and also upon the servants
and upon the handmaids in those days will I pour
out my Spirit" (Joel ii. 28, 29). This prophecy
being expressly fulfilled in the baptism of the Holy

Ghost, doth present that dispensation under the aspect of revelations from the Lord, whether by word, or by vision, or by dream; and gives us to know, that the honour and privilege of being employed as bearers of the mind of God would be greatly extended beyond the measure of former days; would not be restricted to certain persons, families, or schools of the prophets, prepared and set apart of God, but extended to the sons and daughters, the handmaidens and the servants, of the people, yea, unto all flesh — that is, unto all persons, of whatever rank and profession, who feared the Lord and called upon his name. And so it was fulfilled on the day of Pentecost, by coming, not upon the Apostles only, but upon the disciples, women as well as men; and in the case of Cornelius, by coming upon all his kinsmen and near friends (Acts x.): so also upon all the brethren who believed at Ephesus (Acts xix.); and likewise at Samaria (Acts viii.): which being the only four instances recorded, amount to a full proof, that, according to the word of Joel, was the coming of the Spirit "upon all flesh," who believed in the name of Jesus, and were baptized into his body. And by the assurance of receiving the blessing and privilege of this promise Peter did invite the people to come and be baptized, quoting the very words of Joel, "And ye shall receive the gift of the Holy Ghost: for the promise is unto you, and to your children, and to all that are afar off, even as many as the Lord our God shall call" (Acts ii. 38, 39). From this new document, therefore, confirmed by these acts of accomplishment, we learn assuredly that the baptism with the Holy Ghost was intended to generalize and make common that gift of prophecy, vision, and dreams, which had resided in a few chosen and distinguished persons raised up for special occasions; whereby God would preserve in his church every where an infallible voice of truth, and a free discovery of his mind; according to the word of the Lord: "Howbeit, when he, the Spirit of truth, is come, he will guide you into all truth: for he shall not speak of himself; but

whatsoever he shall hear, that shall he speak : and he
will shew you things to come" (John xvi. 13). The
three methods of communication mentioned in Joel
are all supernatural; not by the enlightening of the
reason, or the sharpening of our faculties of discernment, but by express communications from God ;
such as Isaiah received by word, and Daniel by
dreams, and John by visions. Now it is rightly repro-
bated as the vilest infidelity, to assert, as some of the
Germans have dared to do, that the writings of the
Prophets are but the shrewd and sagacious anticipations of wise and good men; against which the
church hath ever maintained, that they should be
reverenced as being to the very word and letter the
inspiration of the Holy Spirit of God, without any intermixture of the mind of those through whose organs
of speech they were delivered ; according to the word
of Balaam, oft repeated : "If Balak would give me
his house full of silver and gold, I cannot go beyond
the commandment of the Lord, to do either good or
bad of mine own mind ; but what the Lord saith,
that will I speak " (Numb. xxiv. 13). Be this allowed,
and I require of every one to believe that the baptism of the Holy Ghost bringeth unto every member
of the Christian church the privilege of conveying
messages from God, with equal pureness, as free from
all intermixture, as the ancient prophets did. For are
not the words, " prophesy," " see visions," " dream
dreams ? " And what is the constant meaning of
these words in the Old Testament, but supernatural
methods by which God was wont to convey his mind,
his own mind and not another's, to the children of
men ? Be assured, then, that the Christian church
ought to be all instinct with supernatural communications ; and that those who now speak amongst us
by the Holy Ghost should be listened to as "the
oracles of God ;" as it is written : " If any man
speak, let him speak as the oracles of God " (1 Pet.
iv. 11).—' And does this living voice supersede the
Scriptures?' No ; by no means.—' And can it contra-
dict the Scriptures ?' Never. If it should, then say,

It is not the Spirit of God, but an unclean spirit which hath spoken. But that there were false prophets in the old time, did not prove that there were not also true ones : no more will it now, if they should again appear.—'And how shall we know them?' Jesus saith, "By their fruits;" Paul, "By their saying that Jesus is the Lord;" John, "By their confessing that Jesus is come in the flesh." We conclude, therefore, that the baptism with the Holy Ghost conveys to the church, and makes common to all the members thereof, those supernatural and extraordinary methods of revelation of which the Old Testament is the offspring.

4. But, besides those methods which God had used in times past for winning the faith of a dark and incredulous world, there was one altogether new and unheard-of, to which he was to set *his* hand as the ultimate resource of his most ingenious benevolence ("and yet for all that will they not hear me, saith the Lord," 1 Cor. xiv. 21): this is, the method of strange tongues, enlarged upon in the chapter of the Corinthians from which we have just quoted; and what we have quoted is taken from the xxviiith chapter of Isaiah, where it lies embosomed in a prophecy to which our Lord makes frequent reference, and sometimes expressly citeth, as also doth the Apostle Paul. For it is to be observed, that the xxviiith and xxixth chapters of Isaiah are but one strain of prophecy ; the one part applicable to the judgments on the whole nation, the other upon Jerusalem in particular. This new method of Divine communication is by enforcing the prophet to utter in a tongue unknown to himself the words which God would carry to the people. And because the people also were, except in an accidental case, as at Pentecost, unacquainted with the voice, there was added, in order to convey the substance and meaning of the same, a gift of interpretation, which sometimes was possessed by the speakers and sometimes by others. But that the speaking with tongues was only a *method* of prophecy, and subsidiary thereto, a

work of God's for shewing that the word was entirely of himself, is manifest from this, that when it fell out upon the day of Pentecost the Apostle Peter said, "This is that which was spoken by the Prophet Joel." And accordingly we find, in all the instances which in divers places have now occurred of this gift, that the person doth only, as it were, introduce his discourse with some words, or at most sentences, of the unknown tongue, and straightway flows on in a strain of English words, most easy to be understood, uttered with great power, and commonly enforced with frequent repetitions. It is nothing more than prophecy, for which the people are prepared by a few words of an unknown tongue, that they may assuredly know that the power which is upon the speaker is not power of his own, but power of God. Whereas in the old times, of Moses and the Prophets, they had but the mother-tongue in the mouth of the prophet, and were left to gather whether it was from God or not merely by natural discernment and the event; we have a sign given to us in addition thereto, the sign of tongues; that we may not be unbelieving, but believe that God is in the man of a truth, and that we may therefore give the more earnest heed to what shall be spoken by him. Taking, therefore, the gift of tongues as no more than a new form of prophecy, adopted for the greater evidence of the truth as the time drew nigh for the fearful accomplishment of the burdens of the Lord, we derive a new light out of the prophecy of Isaiah as to the end of the prophecy of Joel. Isaiah instructeth us, that when God was wearied with the overflowing iniquities of Israel and Judah, and could make no more of them by means of the book, he devised this novel expedient, and thrust it upon them as a last, and the very last, effort he could make for their salvation. The baptism with the Holy Ghost, therefore, among its other uses, serveth for this also, that it warneth the earth, and is a constant manifestation to it of the hand of the Lord. It openeth a refuge; it discovereth an indwelling God, whose presence is sure salvation. It is after the nature of a seal, agai nst the judgments that are about to fall in. Wherefore also it is called a "sealing" 2 Cor. i. 22 ; and Peter presenteth it under the same aspect on the day of Pentecost : "And with many other words did he testify and exhort, saying, Save yourselves from th is untoward generation" (Acts ii. 40). With this ligh t, gathered from these sources, if we return back to t he prophecy of Joel, it comes out with a clearness and unity which it had not before ; and is as follows: First, the gift of the Spirit, to endow the whole church with the power of prophesying against the reign of iniquity, and forewarning men of the coming judgments. This is the revelation which God makes to his prophets, and by them unto the people, before any evil befalleth. The church is the intelligent witness of God's doings, by whom he addresseth the guilty nations in the form of word, that they may repent, and save Him from the most painful necessity of pleading against them by judgments. Then to this are added visible signs, made to the senses, before that fearful and terrible day of the Lord come: "And I will shew wonders in the heavens and in the earth, blood, and fire, and pillars of smoke : the sun shall be turned into darkness, and the moon into blood, before the great and terrible day of the Lord come" (Joel ii. 30, 31). And all this forewarning and prefiguration is for the gracious end of saving and delivering all those who will hear, and behold, and understand, and repent. For it is immediately added, "And it shall come to pass, that whosoever shall call on the name of the Lord shall be delivered : for in Mount Sion and in Jerusalem shall be deliverance, as the Lord hath said, and in the remnant whom the Lord shall call" (ver. 32). Now it so happened, that, just before the awful perdition came upon the Jewish nation, God did, for the sake of warning, and, if it were possible, saving them, fulfil all this prophecy so far as that nation went ; even as the Lord also in the days of his flesh declared that he would do: "Wherefore, behold, I send unto you prophets, and

wise men, and scribes: and some of them ye shall
kill and crucify; and some of them shall ye scourge
in your synagogues, and persecute them from city to
city: that upon you may come all the righteous
blood shed upon the earth, from the blood of righteous Abel unto the blood of Zacharias son of Bara-
chias, whom ye slew between the temple and the
altar. Verily I say unto you, All these things shall
come upon this generation" (Matt. xxiii. 34—36).
And in like manner I do believe that at this present
time, when he is just about to come in judgment
upon all the nations of the earth, in what way is declared in the iiid chapter of Joel, he hath begun to
revive the gift of prophesying with tongues; and will
not cease, through our faith and faithfulness, until,
by means of his prophets speaking with tongues, he
have sent the voice of his warning through every
region of the earth; and, along with it, those wonderful signs in the sun, moon, and stars of heaven,
in the earth, and seas, and nations, which are every
where written as about to precede and usher in the
day of his appearing. And all this work of won-
drous words and signs is done in the long suffering
of God, who " willeth not that any should perish, but
that all should come to repentance" (2 Pet. iii. 9).
We conclude, therefore, from this additional document, that the baptism of the Holy Ghost is the ex-
treme and utmost effort of God to save men from that
day of wrath and perdition which will come upon
all the workers of iniquity; and if this be despised
and blasphemed—as from what hath taken place already we fear will be lamentably the case—then it is
the blasphemy against the Holy Ghost, the last act
of wickedness, in rejecting the last resource of salvation, and which therefore can be forgiven neither in
this world nor in that which is to come.

5. The last two prophetical anticipations of the
baptism with the Holy Ghost hold it up as the channel of communication, by methods supernatural, of
God's holy mind for the salvation of men: that which
we are now to adduce is the recovery and restoration

of the natural channel of reasonable discourse; the enlightening of the mind; the renewing of the will; the purifying of the heart; and the ordering of the speech and conversation in such wise as that God's own mind shall in every thing shine forth as surely and purely as if God, and none but he, were the worker of it all. Now, though the method in this case be not manifestly supernatural, it is as much, and if any thing still more, a Divine work, a work superhuman; inasmuch as it is not occasional, but perpetual infallibility of thought, speech, and behaviour. This was evidenced in the ministry of Christ, who spake with no tongues, and to whom the word of the Lord came not occasionally in the way of prophecy; but who in all things, and at all times, was the Word and the Wisdom of God, and could ever say, "The word which you hear is not mine, but the Father's, which sent me." That prophecy which carries the assurance of this excellent restauration and infallible sustentation of the mind and word of man, through the baptism with the Holy Ghost, is contained in the lxist chapter of Isaiah, and applied by the Lord to himself at the outset of his public ministry (Luke iv. 18), and declared by the Apostle Peter to have been the fruit, not of his spiritual generation, but of the baptism with which he was baptized from heaven at Bethabara beyond Jordan (Acts x. 38). "The Spirit of the Lord God is upon me; because the Lord hath anointed me to preach good tidings unto the meek: he hath sent me to bind up the broken-hearted, to proclaim liberty to the captives, and the opening of the prison to them that are bound; to proclaim the acceptable year of the Lord" (Isai. lxi. 1, 2). It was this anointing which fitted and enabled him for his public ministry; as John the Baptist also declareth: "For he whom God hath sent speaketh the words of God; for God giveth not the Spirit by measure unto him" (John iii. 34). This anointing with the oil of gladness above his fellows was what enabled him to be God's prophet of all truth, and to speak as never man spake. In what this unction did consist, is particularly set forth in another prophecy of Isaiah, concerning the humble and lowly Branch from the root of Jesse: " And the Spirit of the Lord shall rest upon him, the spirit of wisdom and understanding, the spirit of counsel and might, the spirit of knowledge, and of the fear of the Lord ; and shall make him of quick understanding in the fear of the Lord " (Isaiah xi. 2, 3). This is exactly parallel with the prophecy on which we are commenting; and both have a second and after-portion, concerning the day of vengeance and judgment upon the wicked ; which, however, the Lord refrained from quoting in the synagogue of Nazareth, because it was not then fulfilled in their ears, nor shall be until he come again. We have not time to examine these several gifts or attributes of the Divine reason one by one, nor is it needful in this place : suffice it, that they appertain by natural constitution to the soul of man, though they were never till the day of Christ's baptism possessed and occupied by the Holy Spirit. They were created in Adam, and survive in us still, all tenanted by the spirit of evil; which to cast out, and to sweep and garnish the house, the Son of God became incarnate ; and having prevailed to expel the wicked one, he was filled with the Holy Ghost, and so accomplished for his high office of being the Prophet of God, in whom " dwelleth all the treasures of wisdom and knowledge." This treasure he dispenseth to his people by the same Spirit, " He is made unto us wisdom from God ;" and the two very first gifts of the Spirit are, " the word of wisdom, and the word of knowledge"—that is, such an information of the mind by the Holy Ghost as shall possess it with all wisdom and knowledge, and banish from it all ignorance and folly, and accompany the infallible consciousness of truth with a corresponding word or utterance. This is beautifully expressed as an office of the Spirit in the cxxxixth Psalm : " For there is not a word in my tongue, but, lo, O Lord, thou knowest it altogether " (ver. 4). And that it is the privilege and prerogative of every believer, and not

of the Pope only, or a general council, is declared
in these words: " But ye have an unction from the
Holy One, and ye know all things.....But the anointing which ye have received of him abideth in you:
and ye need not that any man teach you: but as
the same anointing teacheth you of all things, and
is truth, and is no lie, and even as it hath taught
you, ye shall abide in him" (1 John ii. 20—27).
Adam was the possessor of fallible reason, the Second
Adam is the possessor of infallible reason; the life
of the first Adam was no security to his members
against ignorance and error, the life of the Second
Adam is. And this difference cometh not from redemption alone, but from inhabitation of God consequent upon incarnation: it pertains not to the Son
of Man under the law, but to the Son of Man baptized with the Holy Ghost: it is not of the human,
but the superhuman; it is the human filled with God
through the incarnation of the Son and the inhabitation of the Father. And therefore, though to appearance it be not so extraordinary and supernatural
as speaking with tongues and prophesying, it is in
fact rather more so, inasmuch as it is constant and
perpetual, and the sure mark of perfectness; according
to the word of James: " If any man offend not in word,
the same is a perfect man, and able also to bridle the
whole body" (James iii. 2). And the same Apostle,
in the same chapter, doth teach us that there is a
wisdom which is from above, as well as a wisdom
which is of the earth: " But the wisdom that is
from above is first pure, then peaceable, gentle, and
easy to be entreated, full of mercy and good fruits,
without partiality, and without hypocrisy" (ver. 17);
which if any man lack, he requireth of him to ask
without doubting: " If any of you lack wisdom, let
him ask of God, that giveth to all men liberally, and
upbraideth not; and it shall be given him. But let
him ask in faith, nothing wavering" (James i. 5, 6).
There can be no doubt, therefore, that to be filled
with God's mind in the inward parts, and to speak it
with simplicity and truth, appertaineth to the bap-

tism of the Holy Ghost, and is thereof one of the
chief, yea, the very chiefest gift, though it have no
extraordinary sign or mark to recognise it by; also,
that this is what especially, and above every other, fits
a man for bearing witness, being that with which
Christ was anointed in order to constitute him " the
faithful and true Witness." And to this, rather than
to any extraordinary prophetic utterances, it is, that
our Lord referreth in the following commandment to
his disciples, when they should be called to bear his
name before kings: " And when they bring you unto
the synagogues, and unto magistrates and powers,
take ye no thought how or what thing ye shall answer, or what ye shall say; for the Holy Ghost shall
teach you in the same hour what ye ought to say"
(Luke xii. 11, 12).

To conclude this promise in one word : I believe,
with St. Paul, that the natural man, not the *sinful*
but the *natural* man, in all his goodliness, as Adam
was created (1 Cor. xv. 45, 46), is not able to receive
the things of the Spirit of God, because they are
spiritually discerned (1 Cor. ii.) ; and that a man
must be born again of the Spirit before he can apprehend the hidden wisdom of God, and utter it
aright. This spiritual generation Christ had from
his conception, being from that time a prepared
vessel, under proof and trial ; and he kept himself a
prepared vessel, not suffering that evil one to touch
him; and into that vessel God poured all the fulness
of wisdom and knowledge at his baptism. So by
regeneration we are prepared for being containers of
the spiritual treasures, which have been hid in God
from the beginning of the world, and which even
" before the world God ordained for our glory ;" to
know things hid from the princes of this world; which
to us are not otherwise revealed than by the Spirit of
the Father, " for the Spirit searcheth all things, yea,
the deep things of God."

6. There remaineth only another of those Old-
Testament prophecies which we have a Divine warrant for applying unto the baptism of the Holy Ghost.

The warrant is given in one of our Lord's utterances which he lifted up in the temple on the last and great day of the Feast of Tabernacles, when it was the custom to bring a golden pitcher of pure water from the pool of Siloam and pour it out upon the victim laid in order upon the altar. On that day, the eighth day of the feast, symbolical of the eternal period consequent upon the Millennium, which is the seventh; perhaps during the very occurrence of that act symbolical of the waters drawn forth from the Shiloh, or Sent One (*Siloam*, " which is by interpretation *Sent* "), in order to complete and perfect the sacrifice, for the libation was always the last thing done unto the sacrifice: at such a time " Jesus stood and cried, saying, If any man thirst, let him come unto me, and drink. He that believeth on me, as the Scripture hath said, out of his belly shall flow rivers of living water. But this spake he of the Spirit, which they that believe on him should receive: for the Holy Ghost was not yet given; because that Jesus was not yet glorified " (John vii. 37—39). It is easier to understand what our Lord meaneth by this, than to ascertain what part of the Scriptures he referreth to; if, indeed, he do refer to any particular place, and not generally to all those places where the Spirit is promised under the emblem of waters; as Isaiah xii. 3, which was wont to be sung on this occasion; Isaiah xxxii. 15, which refers to the time when he shall pour his Spirit upon all the people, and give unto them a clean heart; Isaiah xliv. 3, " For I will pour water upon him that is thirsty, and floods upon the dry ground; I will pour my Spirit upon thy seed, and my blessing upon thine offspring," &c. &c. The emblem of water was so connected with the " times of refreshing from the presence of the Lord," that when John claimed neither to be that Christ, nor Elias, nor that Prophet, they said, " Why then baptizest thou with water ?" But none of these passages contain the idea of the Spirit flowing out of the belly of him that believeth, like water from a fountain—a figure which our Lord useth not only in

H

this place, but also in his discourse with the Samaritan woman (John iv. 14). This is a most material addition to the figure, signifying, that not by outward effusion, but by inward inhabitation, inexhaustible upspringing and plentiful outpouring, would the Spirit be given by him. I know not from what portion of the Scripture the Lord taketh this part of the figure. The following passage of the book of Proverbs, expresseth it perfectly: " The words of a man's mouth are as deep waters, and the well-spring of wisdom as a flowing brook " (Prov. xviii. 4). The same idea, in connection with words the utterance of the Spirit, is thus expressed by Elihu: " For I am full of matter; the Spirit within me constraineth me. Behold, my belly is as wine which hath no vent; it is ready to burst, like new bottles " (Job xxxii. 18, 19). But perhaps the following passage of Isaiah is still more in point: " The Lord shall guide thee continually, and satisfy thy soul in drought, and make fat thy bones: and thou shalt be like a watered garden, and like a spring of water whose waters fail not " (Isaiah lviii. 11). " Flowing out of the belly," is the same as flowing out of the inward parts, the heart, the reins, the spirit; or, in one word, the inward, the spiritual, or hidden parts. The idea of baptism, or washing with water, as connected with the body of Christ, and of " drinking," as connected with the Spirit, is beautifully expressed in the Epistle to the Corinthians, when treating expressly of this very subject: " For by one Spirit are we all baptized into one body, whether we be Jews or Gentiles, whether we be bond or free; and have been all made to drink into one Spirit" (1 Cor. xii. 13). The new information conveyed to us by the Lord's thus alluding to the baptism with the Holy Ghost as a fountain of living waters stricken forth from the flinty heart of man, and flowing out in everlasting streams of utterance, is very important, inasmuch as it teacheth us that the Divine presence, dwelling in the temple of the church, would shew itself thence, and proceed forth in streams of living waters to refresh the barrenness of the earth and heal the waters of the sea (Exod. xlvii.). The Holy Ghost is that river full of waters, so oft spoken of in those Scriptures which refer to the latter times (Psalms xlvi. lxv. &c.), through whose fertilizing power it is that all nature shall put on her rich and beautiful garments. And because the church is a first-fruit of the redeemed creatures, she doth possess, and should ever be serving forth, these waters of refreshment, in the way of instruction, consolation, and blessing, of healing help and holy government. "As every man hath received the gift, even so minister the same one to another, as good stewards of the manifold grace of God" (1 Pet. iv. 10). The type of it was given in the rock, from whose rent side the waters flowed that fed and cleansed the children of Israel in the wilderness; "which Rock was Christ;" and the waters issuing from it are the Holy Ghost flowing from the body of Christ. It is signified, therefore, that not only should we be fed from Christ, but that we should be constituted feeders of others, with the Holy Ghost; and fulfil, as the spouse of Christ, that office which is proper to the mother and the nurse. And here again we fall in with the truth set forth in the fourth particular, of our being ministers or distributers of the Holy Spirit. The complete symbol is in the human body; whose life standeth not in the circulating life of the blood alone, but in a life proper and peculiar to every organ—the heart, the liver, the kidneys, &c.—in virtue of which they do all separate from the circulating blood each a certain portion proper to itself, which they use in building up the body from childhood, and repairing its waste in manhood. Such organs in the church are apostles, prophets, evangelists, pastors, teachers, healers, helps, powers, speakers with tongues, &c.; every one drawing from Christ some portion of his manifold virtue, and pouring it forth from themselves for the perfecting of the saints, for the work of the ministry, for the edifying of the body of Christ.

Such was the state of the revelation concerning the baptism with the Holy Ghost at the time when the forerunner of Jesus announced the Person under whose hand that new administration was to proceed. In opening which, though we have, to keep away all objections, confined ourselves to those texts which by Divine warrant are affixed to that subject, yet would it be a foolish nicety if we did not now declare, upon the analogy of these and parallel texts, that all those passages of Scripture which refer to the consolation of Israel, the new-covenant condition of the Jews and the nations under them, of the world, and of all things, have reference to this subject; and are to be accomplished by the supernatural operation of the Spirit, teaching all men to know the Lord, from the least even to the greatest; by the purification and cleansing of the flesh with water—that is, the sanctification of the body; and by the sending of the river of God through every region of creation : wherefore, also, the days in which these things shall be accomplished are called the "days of refreshing from the presence of the Lord." The baptism of the Spirit poured out upon the church at the day of Pentecost was part and parcel of that work which shall proceed from on high, when the heavens shall contain Jesus no longer ; the earnest of that full reward of power and glory which he shall bring with him ; the first-fruits of that perennial harvest with which all nature shall thenceforward and for ever teem spontaneous. The superhuman powers presently possessed by the church are but glimpses of the glory which is yet to be revealed ; a continual witness of that power and manner of working throughout all nature with which Jesus is to come attended ; which God is then to put forth in the church, and from his holy temple, the church, to disperse through the various departments of creation, both invisible and visible. The prognostication and description of this blessed estate is not the subject of a few isolated texts of the Old Testament, but the burden of all the Prophets, the theme of all the Psalms, and the end of all the types and symbols of the Law. The one object of prophecy is to discover to the groaning, travailing creature the sure and certain hope of its deliverance from the bondage of corruption ; and to ensure unto men the sovereignty of the renewed and blessed world, in reward of our patient endurance of the afflictions and penalties of sin, and of our earnest contention against the prince and ruler of the darkness. And being so, instead of selecting a few passages, we might have quoted and commented upon half, and more than half, of all the prophetical word and symbolical institutions of the Old Testament, as pertaining to our subject, and containing the perfection and completeness of that supernatural work of the Holy Ghost, both over mind and over matter, whereof his baptism is the firstfruits and earnest. But because it is only the firstfruits and earnest whereof we have undertaken to discourse, and because we would pillar our argument upon Divine warranty, we have thought it better to limit ourselves to these six notices, which beyond all question refer to this subject. And now we proceed to examine what further light the Gospels cast upon the matter ; for they also speak prophetically in respect to the baptism of the Holy Ghost, which became not fact of history until the day of Pentecost, after that Jesus was taken up into his glory.

II. From the time that Zacharias, the father of John, received the heavenly message that Messiah's forerunner was to be the son of his and his wife's old age, the whole narrative makes us to feel that we are arrived at a new era in the history of God's dealings, which is the era of the fulness of the Holy Ghost. For, whereas in the Old Testament the calling of the prophets and the utterances of their burdens are ascribed to the word of the Lord which came to them, from this time forth every one of God's communications through men is ascribed to their being filled with the Holy Ghost. In the very annunciation of John's birth and ministry he is destined of God to " be filled with the Holy Ghost, even from his mother's womb ;" and it is as a *spiritual* Elias, " in the spirit and power of Elias," that he is to go before the Christ. At the annunciation of Messiah himself,

H 3

made to the blessed Virgin, the work of his generation is by the " Holy Ghost, and the power of the
Most High ;" in virtue of which he should call and
enjoy God for his Father: " Therefore he shall be
called the Son of God." These three things, " the
Holy Ghost," " the power of the Highest," and
" the Fatherhood of God," answering to the three
great titles of our subject, the " baptism with the Holy
Ghost," the " promise of the Father," and " power
from on high," do meet together in the supernatural generation. When the two mothers accost one another,
each bearing her precious burden—the one, the Word
made flesh; the other, the Baptist filled with the Holy
Ghost—Elizabeth speaks out with a loud voice, " being filled with the Holy Ghost," and the blessed
Virgin maketh reply, in a canticle which the church
hath ever received as a perfect utterance of the
Holy Ghost, though not positively declared to be so.
And after the Baptist's birth, when they came together to circumcise him, his father's tongue was un-
loosed, and he was " filled with the Holy Ghost and
prophesied." And when the child Jesus was brought
forth and circumcised, and they took him to present
him in the temple, the Lord of the temple had prepared old Simeon to welcome and bless the child, by
putting the Holy Ghost upon him, and revealing
things to him by the Holy Ghost, and giving him
utterance in the power of the same prophetic Spirit.
These instances, occurring in the narrative of one
year's transactions, do bespeak the opening of a new
dispensation, the dispensation of the Holy Ghost. It
is not by the Word coming unto them; for the Word
was now become himself a needy mortal, restricted
within the confines of a conceived child, and therefore can no more come or go personally otherwise than
in this fleshly form. He is now under the senses of
men, himself the Son of Man; not capable of multiplying his presence; busy with the work of sanctifying
himself, and overcoming the devil; and he is therefore no longer the prime mover, but the obedient
sufferer; and every thing proceeds under the hand

of the Holy Ghost. The Father created the world,
and provideth for it; and after the Fall doth constitute it under the present condition of death. The
Son doth straightway propound the redemption, and
disclose it in all ways of word and action, and make
the world, and especially the Jewish people, ready
for it; crowning all his labours of preparation by
stripping Himself of his glory, and coming himself to be the Father's sacrifice, as Isaac to Abra-
ham. Then the Holy Ghost taketh up the mighty
work, and bringeth the self-sacrificed Son into the
condition of a mortal child, making the right and
due preparations: Christ always submitting, He
always receiving his self-emptiedness, and clothing
him anew with anointed life, according to the Father's
mind; first with vile garments, afterwards with glorious ones; first with humiliation, afterwards with exaltation: and under the same hand of the Holy Ghost
proceedeth the sanctification and the salvation of the
church, and shall proceed the glorification of the creatures. This is the reason why, from the opening of the
New Testament, every thing is said to be done by the
Holy Ghost; through whom God is giving testimony
concerning, and making due preparation for, his Son.

The work of the Holy Ghost, thus auspiciously
begun upon the fallen creation, the Baptist, when
ripened by the Spirit for his stern ministry, cometh
forth out of the wilderness and announceth as about
to proceed under the hand of Jesus of Nazareth,
the Son of God. The mighty work of building
God's living temple; preparing God's body for action, his organ for speech, and his hand for rule
and government; the mighty work of re-producing
all creation from its bed of death, and conveying
it into the state of divine inhabitation and infallible
blessedness; John the Baptist announceth as about
to be done under the hand of a mortal man in
our flesh and blood, circumcised unto the obedi-
dience of the Law, baptized into the liberty of the
Gospel, and submissive to the duties of both, calling
Jehovah his God and Father. Man is to ransom

man from death, and to inform with everlasting life
man's fallen and ruined habitation. And why so?
Because God made man to be his image and likeness,
in and through whom all that ever should be seen
and known and felt of God, by all creatures, should
come to them, and abide with them; and for this
other reason, that by his Son, acting within the limits
of the Christ, or risen God-man, creation had been
ordered, and so therefore must be governed, restored
and glorified and blessed for ever. The work which
the Baptist announced as about to proceed under
the hand of Jesus of Nazareth is twofold: first, to
baptize with the Holy Ghost; and, secondly, to
baptize with fire: the former set on foot at Pentecost,
and still continuing, and to be completely accomplished in the glorification of the church without
spot or wrinkle or any such thing; the latter beginning thereupon, in the coming of Christ with all his
saints in flaming fire, to purge out all iniquity from
the created universe, and cast out into hell all wicked
spirits and wicked men, there to abide in the misery
and impotence of the second death for ever and ever.
This work being completed, the created world is
lifted into its blessed rest for ever; and God, dwelling
in the church, and through the church speaking
and acting, doth communicate with the blessed creation both as to giving and receiving—giving to it his
good and perfect gifts, and from it receiving its
willing homage, thanks, and praise. It is only the
former of these works which we inquire into; and this
the Baptist declareth is to be done under the hand of
Jesus of Nazareth, who may therefore well be expected to be himself the great Prophet of the work
which he is to perform; for "no one knoweth the
Father but the Son," who knoweth him even as he
himself is known of the Father. Forasmuch as it is
the promise of the Father which is in question, we
may surely look to be fully informed thereof only
from the Son's own mouth. And so we find those
prophetic anticipations to be but hints and notices,
when compared with the plentiful information which

is contained in the words and works of our Lord upon this subject, which we have taken in hand to set forth in order.

1. And first, in general, we present the whole public ministry of our blessed Lord, both as respects his discourses and his mighty deeds, his words and his works, as the manifestation at large, so far as they go, of the baptism with the Holy Ghost with which he was anointed in the form of a dove. And this we do on the authority of his own declaration in the synagogue of Nazareth (Luke iv. 18—22), referred to above; and of the Apostle Peter's declaration to Cornelius, in these words: "The word which God sent unto the children of Israel, preaching peace by Jesus Christ (he is Lord of all): that word, I say, ye know, which was published throughout all Judea, and began from Galilee, after the baptism which John preached: how God anointed Jesus of Nazareth with the Holy Ghost and with power; who went about doing good, and healing all that were oppressed of the devil: for God was with him" (Acts x. 36—38). This passage distinctly referreth both the word of Christ's preaching and the works of his power to that anointing which he received after John's baptism; and dates its beginning, not from his generation, birth, infancy, or youth, but from the time he began to preach in Galilee after he had received that heavenly seal and preparation. It is a confusion, therefore, by no means to be permitted, to overlook this destination of the Holy Ghost, and to ascribe it all to the miraculous generation, or, as most do, to his personality as a Divine Person. The glory of his personality is seen in his deigning to become man, and keep himself so; in his willingness to receive all the virtue of a holy human life from his Father in the generation of the Holy Ghost, all the power of witness-bearing and witness-working and God-manifesting in the baptism of the Holy Ghost. Yield to them who please, I am resolved, by God's grace, that those licensed and ordained manufacturers of a Gospel shall never drive me, with all their Babylonish

thunder, from that form and fashion of the Gospel
which the Holy Ghost himself once delivered to the
saints: and being so resolved, I hold to the position,
that not in virtue of the Holy Ghost's generation,
but in virtue of the Holy Ghost's baptism, did Jesus
preach with authority the word of peace, and heal
all that were oppressed with the devil. This most
important point of doctrine is further manifest from
his own frequent declarations to the same effect;
wherein he disclaimeth, yea, and solemnly renounceth,
all power in himself so to speak and so to act; and
referreth it all to his Father's power, the power of
God which abode in him and wrought in him always,
and always wrought him into a perfect image of the
invisible God. For example: "The words that I speak
unto you, I speak not of myself; but the Father, that
dwelleth in me, he doeth the works" (John xiv. 10).
And that these works were not done in him of the
Father in virtue of any thing proper to him as a Divine
Person, but in consequence of his holy manhood and
by means thereof, is manifest from the same works,
yea, and greater, being assured unto all who believe,
in the verses immediately following: "Believe me
that I am in the Father, and the Father in me: or
else believe me for the very works' sake. Verily,
verily, I say unto you, He that believeth on me, the
works that I do shall he do also; and greater works
than these shall he do; because I go unto my Father"
(vers. 11, 12). As to what these greater works are,
we have some insight given us in the following
passage, which is equally strong as to the leading
question now before us: "Verily, verily, I say unto
you, The Son can do nothing of himself, but what
he seeth the Father do: for what things soever he
doeth, these also doeth the Son likewise. For the
Father loveth the Son, and sheweth him all things
that himself doeth: and he will shew him greater
works than these, that ye may marvel. For as the
Father raiseth up the dead, and quickeneth them;
even so the Son quickeneth whom he will. For the
Father judgeth no man, but hath committed all judg-

ment unto the Son: that all men should honour the Son, even as they honour the Father" (John v. 19—23). These "greater works" are concerned with his coming again to judge the quick and the dead; wherein we shall also share with him, as we now share with him in those words and works which flow from the baptism of the Holy Ghost. I will venture to assert, that there is not one discourse of our Lord's recorded in the Gospel by John, wherein he doth not assert this great truth, " that the doctrine was not his own, but the Father's which sent him ;" " that he did not speak of himself, but the Father, which sent him, gave him commandment what he should say and what he should speak ;" "that of himself he could do nothing." For he came to be a witness, and not a principal; and his work was accomplished when he had borne full and perfect witness unto the Father's mind and power. This was the way in which he had undertaken to glorify the Father, by hiding himself, by making himself of no reputation ; and if he seemed to be wise, and merciful, and mighty, to disclaim it as his own, and ascribe the glory of it unto the Father dwelling in him. Thus Jesus at once revealed the creature's nothingness, and God's all-sufficiency in it for good, for the victory over sin and the devil and death.

If, then, we would see the baptism of the Holy Ghost laid out at large, and embodied in a various and busy life, we must look at the ministry of Jesus ; and be assured, that all which he spake and all which he did, up to the measure of infallibility in the one, and raising the dead in the other, the baptism with the Holy Ghost doth enable and require the church to perform. It is not blasphemy, but it is duty, to believe and assert that the believer is called upon to walk in the footsteps of Jesus in all respects, speaking at all times as he spake, and working as he also wrought. "These signs shall follow them that believe: In my name shall they cast out devils ; they shall speak with new tongues ; they shall take up serpents ; and if they drink any deadly thing it shall not hurt them ; they shall lay hands on the sick, and they shall recover " (Mark xvi. 17, 18). What a shame and what a crime it is, then, that the church of the believers should be found in the state in which it is ; speaking all different opinions, exercising no infallible discernment of truth, and putting forth no signs whatever—in one word, making Jesus a liar, and counting it glorious to do so! I am ashamed, verily I am confounded, on account of our sin ; and will open my mouth in confession and lamentation, until the Lord shall have taken away this our reproach, and made us to cease to be a reproach unto Christ.

Whenever Jesus, therefore, speaks of the Holy Ghost in his discourses, he speaks of that which had not only been announced in the Old Testament, from the beginning, as the unspeakable gift of God to the church, and the glorious consummation of all blessedness to the creation ; but which had also been exemplified in himself, and was to be exemplified in his resurrection, and exaltation, his coming again in glory and judging the wicked, and settling all things in eternal blessedness ;—exemplified, inwardly, in the work of faith through his generation staying the alienation, and hastening away of all nature from God, and keeping him in the Father, that the Father might be in him ; outwardly, in the word of all wisdom and all knowledge, which he spake with the infallibility of God ; in the work of all mercy and power, which he wrought with the omnipotence of God. When Jesus in his discourses maketh promise of the Holy Ghost to his church, it is of that Person whose manner and strength of working had been exemplified in his own case, by bringing his nature holy out of an unholy mother, by preserving it holy, by filling it with the light and life of God, by giving it the infallible utterance of God, and empowering it to work the holy and mighty works of God. He was the thing which he promised that they should be, in virtue of the baptism with the Holy Ghost ; whose manner of working changeth not, his force of working abateth not, but is

ever able, as he is ever sent, to conform us in all respects unto that image which Christ shewed upon the
earth.

1. The true use to make of the life and ministry of
the word and work of the Son of Man, is, therefore,
this: As the model of the man baptized with the
Holy Ghost, unto which all who afterwards should
be in like manner baptized, are to be conformed.
In all things he must have the pre-eminence; and in
this also, of shewing forth the holy manner and operation of fallen mortal flesh when baptized with the
Holy Ghost. To him it appertained, not only to
bear the burden and penalty of a transgressed law,
and to overcome the curse of death, but also to receive and to occupy; with God's own husbandry to
economize, and for God's own ends to dispense, the
new endowment of power from on high, with which
our nature was now to be gifted. He must not only
see us out of the narrow straits into which we had
brought ourselves, but also navigate before us the open
seas, through which we must win our way to our eternal
safety and rest. This is what he did after his baptism: he, being man, shewed forth in all human life
and action the manner of the Holy Ghost's operation, exactly as God would have it always to be shewn
forth; and without such a prototype, we should have
been all at sea in respect to what is right and proper
in persons so endowed. But having Jesus' ministry
of the Holy Ghost before us, we dare say to every
one thus gifted, Thou must carry thyself after this
model, and thou must take no liberty to deviate
from it in any particular. And thus all hypocrisy
and false pretences are detected, all fanaticism and
superstition prevented, in this superhuman, and therefore mysterious, region of the Christian calling. We
can say, the most illiterate and weak of the con-
gregation can say, and ought to say, to the most
gifted, Thou must make no deviation from the footsteps of Jesus, in the use of those thy superhuman
and celestial gifts; thou must not claim upon thy
Divine commission to depart in spirit or in act from

I

him who first fulfilled that commission. The spirit
of the prophets is subject to the prophets; and therefore thou must bring thy power and gift, whatever it
is, to be conformed to Jesus ; and from this way thou
must not flinch one iota to the right hand or to the
left, without confessing it to be sin, and departing
from it with all haste : and thus it is that the Spirit
testifies to Jesus, thus that the gift is subservient to
the Lord of the gift, thus that the baptized acknowledge the Baptizer with the Holy Ghost. I cannot
proceed from this remark onward to its applications,
without saying that I deem it to be the most important practical observation which I have made ; and
if my reader see it not in this light, I commend it to
him to read it over and over until it so appear. For
without both the understanding and the application
of Christ's ministry of the Holy Ghost as a model
to all the baptized therewith, I perceive that the gifts
now bestowing upon the church will not be without
peril and evil, as at Corinth, and that Satan will gain
an advantage over us.

2. Now, then, let us see what in Jesus the baptism
with the Holy Ghost led to ; how that superhuman
inspiration moved and actuated this man. And first,
negatively : It did not move him to violate any of the
ties and obligations of nature, so as that he should
not be bound to honour father and mother, to keep
covenant between man and man, and, in one word,
to love his neighbour as himself; nor to break any
ordinance of the law, of which he was ever most
observant. Because creation, as hath been said, is
an effect and operation of the Spirit, and so is that
most holy law of God: now the Spirit will not in his
highest operation make void his lower ones, but always
act consistent and harmonious with himself. Yet the
higher unction did deliver the lower from the erroneous misapplication which man had made of them ;
for example, postponing the second table of the Law
to the first, and requiring us to hate father and mother, and ourselves, for the love of God ; also, bringing the positive under the moral, by ever submitting

the letter of the commandment to the spirit of the commandment, teaching that to do good is the end, the Sabbath and every ordinance but the means. If Jesus seem to violate any ordinance of God, it is only in appearance: study the action closer, and you will find that he is retrieving the law from a use of bondage into the right use of liberty, and so making it honourable. For the complete work which he accomplished was not to annihilate the creation work, but to redeem it by evacuating the law of sin in the flesh; not to make void the law, but by the Spirit to enable us to fulfil the righteousness thereof. I say, therefore, that the baptism with the Holy Ghost can never set aside a creature obligation or a moral duty, but will establish them, and give them to be enjoyed as true liberty: and therefore, so far from hindering charity, the superhuman gift is for the end of charity given to every one to profit withal.

3. Again, negatively, this baptism did not set aside any obligation to the church, or to the state, of all which, even unto the paying of tribute, and the reverencing of those murderers who sat in Moses' seat, Jesus was most observant; and so were his Apostles who swerved not, until the temple fell, and the ritual fell along with it, from any even of the ceremonial observances, as both Paul's example and his protestation do certify (Acts xviii. xx). This is a most important observation as bearing upon the present state of the churches, which are altogether or almost such as Satan would have them to be; and yet we are not to lift hand against them, or wittingly to offend them, but simply to go on with Christ's work in all its bearings; and if they cast us out, still to go on with Christ's work all the same as if nothing had happened. To prefer to obey Christ to the obeying of the king, is not to dishonour the king, but to do our duty both by the king and the Christian; so also to serve Jesus against the verdict of the church, is at once to acquit us of our obligations and to remind the church of hers. Allegiance to the king and submission to the church, is not to surrender our conscience up to

them, which is the Lord's own right who purchased
and purified it with his blood, but to bear patiently
with their frown, exaction, and excommunication,
and take no arms, and make no resistance, but still
persevere in preferring the word of the King of kings,
the supremacy of the Head of the church. But,
while the Holy Ghost doth continue to prompt us
with a straightforward course, to the honour of
Jesus and his lordship, it prevents us from setting
up any adverse faction or sect, carrying arms against,
or plotting in any way the subversion of, the powers
that be established, whether in the church or in the
state. If we suffer, we suffer as Christians meekly
for the truth's sake, and we carry on our Christian
testimony and action until our course is ended by
persecution and death. These two negative effects
of the Holy Ghost's baptism I have deemed it good
to place first, because it hath been so much the
custom to plead a super-human commission for the
violation of things honest, and true, and pure, and of
good report, and for the pulling down of things established. And I feel assured the same thing will be
attempted of Satan again, to mar this beautiful and
blessed work of the Lord which is now proceeding.

4. We would now set forth *positively* what the
baptism of the Holy Ghost did enable Christ to perform, above and beyond the measure of redeemed
and regenerated manhood, which he had already,
being generated of the Spirit, and continued to have,
anterior to his baptism. And, first, being a new
trust and consignment from the Creator to the creature, it brought its own powers of husbandry along
with it. It came not upon man for the purpose of
loading him with a new duty and obligation of ministering the Spirit, without at the same time bringing power from God to enjoy and rightly minister
the same; not for a burden, but for a strengthening;
not for an oppression, but an enjoyment. Its operation was first in the will, to endue it with new reso-
lution and strength for the new work which was to
be done. Now this is to say no more than that it

was spiritual; for whatever is spiritual hath its seat in the will or spirit of man, and thence circulates outward through the mind and understanding and sense and visible world. There is an invisible and there is a visible world. Man was made and set up in Adam as the lord of the former; man came to be in Christ the lord of the latter. By creation he was the germ of the spiritual, the completeness of the natural, lord; by incarnation, or spiritual generation, he came to be the spiritual lord; but before he could be so installed, he must first recover the natural lordship which he had forfeited; and, this done, he is instated therein by baptism of the Holy Ghost. In virtue whereof a power and faculty royal, a prerogative singular and divine, entereth into him, and he is constituted Lord of the spiritual and invisible world, by God's own residence in him as a joyful presence of blessedness, and a glorious omnipotence of power. To talk of a new obligation, without a new power conferred on the creature, is entirely beyond the mark, either of justice or of goodness. But the baptism of the Holy Ghost did bring Jesus into the new obligation of administering superhuman powers more mighty than ten legions of angels; and we must not for a moment suppose that there came not along therewith into his will resolute strength, and firm assurance, equal to the task of using the same for God's glory. Now because all power, whether old or new, is from God, we must conclude that God at this time took up his residence in the human soul or creature will of Christ, after another manner than heretofore he had done. If it be asked, 'After what manner?' I answer, By indwelling of the Father. And if it be asked again, ' But is not incarnation or generation of God the same therewith?' I answer, No; but preparatory thereto. Incarnation is a work, is *the* work of the Son; inhabitation is a work, is *the* work of the Father. Both are works, not in the flesh but in the will; for the flesh is as yet mortal and corruptible, and in the likeness of flesh of sin; but the former is the Son's work of concentrating and humbling himself within the limited powers of a human will, and therein acting unto the redemption of the fleshly creature from the power of sin and corruption, according to the ordinances of the carnal law; the latter is the entering thereinto of God's divine capacity of strength and might, enough to bring, not the physical or natural, but the spiritual and the invisible, under the power of the incarnate Son. The Son would have the honour of redeeming man, the Father would have the honour of bringing all things visible and invisible under the power of the redeemed man; and the Holy Ghost effectuates both works, the former by spiritual generation, the latter by spiritual baptism; which, though they concur and meet together in Christian baptism in the members, stood widely apart as to time in our Head, to the end we might see and know them to be distinct works of the Father and the Son; working in the believer, the one by incorporating union with Christ's body, the other by spiritual indwelling therein. This indwelling of the Father then, I assert, brought positive increase of power to the human will, which it had not by creation, nor hath by spiritual generation, though prepared for it thereby, but hath only through spiritual baptism; and this power was to the end of administering the supremacy of the spiritual and invisible world.

5. In proof of which observe, next, That almost immediately upon his receiving the baptism he was "led up," or "driven," of the Spirit into the wilderness, to be tried of the devil. Three of the Evangelists place this event next after the baptism with the Holy Ghost, shewing us thereby that in the mind and narration of the Spirit, there was a most intimate connection between them; the one being the power communicated, the other the proper trial to which it is put; as a man having built a ship launcheth her straightway upon that element which she is destined to contend with and make use of. And it is only the more evidenced that the baptism was for the subjection of the spiritual world, by the circumstances

that the intervening incidents narrated in the first
chapter of John are omitted, and as it were over-
leaped, by the Spirit in the other three Evangelists, in
order to bring the spiritual baptism and the spiritual
temptation into the closest contact of cause and
effect, of rule and example. Adam was not set in
array against the devil, but against physical nature,
because he was the appointed lord and keeper thereof;
but Christ was set in array against the devil, against
Satan the prince of this world, and all the spiritual
wickednesses in the high places of which he is the so-
vereign lord. Satan did, indeed, intrude himself into
paradise, and thereby contract upon himself fresh guilt;
but he had no power to alter or to modify in any way
God's goodly creatures, but only to speak words in
the hearing of our common mother. In the case of
Christ he had power to wield the world against him,
to whirl him hither and thither through the air, and to
call into the most active play and operation the whole
machinery of the natural and spiritual world. But it
availed not, the baptized Son of Man withstood and
discomfited him, and sent him away broken and
fallen and powerless. And he drove him from the
savage creatures of the wilderness beside which he
abode, and they harmed him not: and the angels
came and ministered to him. Which circumstances
being put together do exhibit to us a perfect example of the virtue of spiritual baptism;—man holy
in his soul and in his flesh; man overcoming and
expelling the devil and his angels; man redeeming
the creatures from their thraldrom of cruelty and
death; man waited on and served by the angels: in
one word, man supreme, both over the natural and
the spiritual; the former to redeem, the latter to
judge and separate, all evil angels to condemn, all
good angels to sustain and to be served by. To the
redemption of the natural, which the Son by incarnation procureth, is added the rule and government
of the spiritual, which the Father by inhabitation
conferreth. Therefore we conclude, that one baptized
with the Holy Ghost is set for the command of good
angels, for the judgment of evil ones; seeing that

from this time forth legions of angels waited the bidding of the Son of Man, and legions of devils fled howling at his command. And the same powers of " casting out devils in his name," of " discerning of spirits," still appertaineth to those who believe, upon whom also the angels attend as " ministering spirits sent forth to minister to them which shall be heirs of salvation." These are high thoughts, and of an infinite range, but I feel that the truth of God is in them : and I see the broken fragments of that truth in the superstitions of all countries, and especially in the legends of saints; whose revenge upon Satan, subjection of his evil imps, and use of holy angels, are constantly recurring in their story. And in virtue of this new region of sovereignty into which the spiritual baptism doth introduce men, it is, that the sin against the Holy Ghost, or the abuse of this wonderful power, is so fearful and utterly unpardonable. Man's fall out of the natural supremacy was retrievable ; but his fall out of the spiritual is utterly irretrievable. The one led to shocking natural sins and corruptions, such as were found exhibited in the heathen world, and are recorded in the first chapter of the Romans and elsewhere : but these are almost nothing when compared with the hideous blasphemies, satanic mockeries, unheard-of heresies, and spiritual delusions, which the apostates from the primitive church fell into, and practised as holy acts of religion, and palmed upon the world as the worship of God and of Christ. And I feel assured that all which then fell out is as nothing when compared with what shall yet be seen, and that immediately, in the Christian church, when the gifts of the Holy Ghost shall have been conferred again, and with them the power of quenching, resisting, and blaspheming the Holy Ghost. Against all which I call upon the saints of God to be ever defended by the power of an indwelling God and Saviour.

6. We observe further, that in consequence of this inhabitation of God in the redeemed and renewed will of man, not only was Jesus able in himself to possess, and from himself to communicate unto others,

" power and authority over all devils, and to cure
diseases," " to tread on serpents and scorpions, and
over all the power of the enemy;" but also he was
strengthened to know and to communicate the whole
mind and will of God. It was not from learning in
the Law and the Prophets, though in these he was
more skilled than the doctors; nor was it from any
superior order of natural endowments, for he was
man after the form and fashion of other men; but
from the illumination and teaching of the Spirit, that
he had such treasures of wisdom and knowledge as
he poured forth upon men, to their wonder and
amazement. " He spake to them as one having authority, and not as the Scribes." " Never man spake
as this man." Not only doth our Lord assert this at
the outset of his ministry (Luke iv.) but on all occasions; as, for example, when the people marvelled :
" How knoweth this man letters, having never learned ?" (John vii. 15.) The way that Jesus took to
make their wonder cease, was by informing them,
that he was taught by the Father, and spake the
Father's doctrine. " Jesus answered them, and said,
My doctrine is not mine, but his that sent me. If
any man will do his will, he shall know of the doctrine, whether it be of God, or whether I speak of
myself" (vers. 16, 17). Again; " When ye have lifted
up the Son of Man, then shall ye know that I am
he, and that I do nothing of myself; but as my Father hath taught me, I speak these things " (viii. 28).
And again, towards the end of his ministry, " For
I have not spoken of myself: but the Father which
sent me, he gave me a commandment, what I should
say and what I should speak. And I know that his
commandment is life everlasting : whatsoever I speak
therefore, even as the Father said unto me, so I
speak " (xii. 49, 50). In all these, and many other
the like passages, I ask what it is that Jesus doth disclaim, if it be not the notion, that in virtue of natural and inherent powers of manhood he spake. He
would have them to understand, that it was not as
the Son of Man, but as the Son of Man sent, sanc-

tified, and commissioned of the Father, and informed of the Father by the Spirit of the Father, that he
taught them these things, which the same Spirit afterwards brought to the mind of his disciples, and
which they recorded for our learning.   As it was with
the Prophets, so was it with Jesus, the great Prophet, and the Confirmer of them all (Rom. xv. 8).
They had the Spirit of Christ in measure, He without
measure.   It is inspiration in both cases; in theirs,
an inspiration ofttimes beyond their own comprehen-
sion (1 Pet. i.); in his, never: in theirs, confined to
a part of wisdom and knowledge ; in his, embracing
the Godhead-fulness thereof. The natural man, taken
at the best, created or redeemed, is not able to apprehend spiritual things, which are both discerned
in the heart by the Spirit, and uttered with the lips
by the same Spirit.   And therefore the first and
highest distributions of the Spirit are " the word of
wisdom," and " the word of knowledge." All preaching of the Gospel is by the Holy Spirit, who alone
can bring things out from the infinite mind of God,
and communicate them without error, through the
faculties and the words of a fallible man.   And that
it was thus with the preaching of Jesus, himself declareth (Luke iv.), and Peter also (Acts x).   And
the reason of this incapacity of man, or any other
finite being, to search the mind of God, is expressly
given by the Apostle in these words : " Eye hath not
seen, nor ear heard, neither have entered into the
heart of man, the things which God hath prepared
for them that love him. But God hath revealed them
unto us by his Spirit: for the Spirit searcheth all
things, yea, the deep things of God.   For what man
knoweth the things of a man, save the spirit of man
which is in him ? even so the things of God knoweth
no man, but the Spirit of God " (1 Cor. ii. 9—11).
And that this extendeth also to the utterance of them,
is with equal plainness declared in the verses following : " Now we have received, not the spirit of the
world, but the Spirit which is of God ; that we might
know the things that are freely given to us of God.

Which things also we speak, not in the words which
man's wisdom teacheth, but which the Holy Ghost
teacheth; comparing spiritual things with spiritual"
(vers. 12, 13), [or, as the last clause is better rendered, " submitting spiritual things to spiritual persons"]. And immediately he declareth, that no force
of natural genius could enable a person to apprehend
these things which the Spirit enabled them to utter.
" But the natural man receiveth not the things of
the Spirit of God : for they are foolishness unto him;
neither can he know them, because they are spiritually discerned. But he that is spiritual discerneth
all things, yet he himself is discerned of no man"
(vers. 14, 15). And, finally, to shew that this Spirit
was the same which inspired Jesus, it is added,
" For who hath known the mind of the Lord, that
he may instruct him? but we have the mind of
Christ" (ver. 16). When Jesus became man under
the law, he grew into the knowledge of the law by
means of the word of God, and astonished all the
doctors with his proficiency; when he was anointed
with the Spirit, he passed out of the region of the
perfect natural man, into the region of the spiritual
man, and became the complete Prophet, the faithful
and true Witness of God, for the communication of
all his mind whatever. There prevaileth, as we have
already observed, a great error upon this subject, as
if Jesus, through his Godhead, gat hold of God's
mind, and without any intervention of the Spirit,
rendered it out unto man in the form of reasonable
discourse. But that view of the subject is not according to the truth of the Trinity, which, even in
the absolute Godhead, doth require that the Spirit
should intercommune between the Father and the
Son ; but still less doth it stand with the doctrine of
the Incarnation, which requireth that the Son be
very man, acting and thinking always within man's
bounds, and that the Holy Spirit carry on the inter-
course between the absolute Godhead of the Father
and the Son, thus restricting himself to the bounds
of manhood. If the Son, having become man, can

out of manhood reach up into the secret bosom of God, and comprehend and reveal the things therein, man is made commensurate with God; and the work of Jesus hath glorified manhood unto God, instead of revealing Godhead in man. But if Jesus, being man, can reveal no truth of God, otherwise than as the Father bringeth it unto him by the Holy Ghost, then is the limitations of manhood ascertained, and his dependence upon God for knowledge, as for every thing besides, is revealed. While at the same time the capacity of the Spirit, and his willingness to make the things of God to be apprehended, and to be uttered by man, is proved beyond all contradiction. The Word which came to the seers and prophets in the former dispensation, in order to manifest himself as the Redeemer of flesh, becomes flesh, and conforms it to the law; and this done, God manifests him as the Head of a new and everlasting dispensation, that of the Holy Ghost, whereof he doth institute a beginning, to serve for a model, in the days of his flesh, and shall exercise the completeness for ever and ever. Being thereby proved to be the Son of God, not only by the creation of the world, and by its redemption, but by its glorification with spiritual and celestial glory of the resurrection, and infallible, state for ever and for ever. And the manner of communication between the two persons in the blessed Trinity, the Father and the Son, is thus brought to light in the sphere of manhood; the Father generative, the Son generated; the Father pouring all his fulness into the generated Son by the Spirit, the Son's loving submissiveness to the Father, even to death; and the Father's cleaving and indivisible union to the Son even in death; the Father's doing of every thing by the Son, and the Son's doing it for the Father;—all by means of the Holy Spirit intervening between them, and bearing through all distance, and over all disparity of assumed condition, the very mind of the Father, and causing it to be exhibited in the Son, just as it is in the Father. I believe it was through reasonings of this kind, that the marvellously exact doctrine of the Trinity, contained in the primitive creeds, was slowly and gradually educed out of the revealed fact of the Incarnation. The doctrine of the Trinity is nothing but the fact of the Incarnation thrown into an attitude of defence against those who said, " But if Jesus was very man, then was he nothing more than man, and surely not God." No, saith the voice of the orthodox church, " Although he is a creature, he is the Creator self-humbled into a creature, and although he is the Spirit-served Man, he is the Spirit-server thus self-humbled to receive service; because, when a few years are over, lo ! he is exalted to be the Governor of all creation, and the Dispenser of all the Spirit's gifts." Other men must all bow to this man in worship, and on him depend for every inspiration of knowledge or of power. Christ's Divinity is a conclusion from his exaltation : " declared to be the Son of God with power, according to the Spirit of holiness, by the resurrection from the dead." Christ's humanity is a conclusion from his humiliation ; and both together are necessary, and alike necessary to be believed for a man's salvation. But perhaps we have gone a little too far from the straight course ; for they will always be crying, Socinianism ! and we are loath that people should have any handle for censure, or occasion of offence. The thing we have been endeavouring to set forth under this particular, is, that the Son of Man was inspired by the Spirit from the Father, in all the wisdom and knowledge which he uttered, and had it not distilled as it were out of his Godhead into his manhood, which mingleth the natures of Christ, and maketh him neither God nor man in his actions, but an amalgam or compound of both, hideth the work both of the Father and the Holy Ghost, and wholly excludes him from being any example to us, and especially from being that model of the spiritual man which we are now setting him forth to have been.

Besides this, the baptism of the Holy Ghost did endow the man Christ Jesus, with superhuman powers over other men, and over the various regions of na-

K

ture, both animate and inanimate. Over other men,
—in the instances, of his Apostles and Disciples,
whom, when it pleased him, he called, and the Spirit
of the Father made them willing;—of the people,
and the very children, who were made willing in the
day of his triumphant entrance into Jerusalem, to
sing, "Hosannah unto the Son of David;" present-
ing a grand type of the willing people who shall hail
him with shouts to his temple, when he shall come
again;—of the man who on the same occasion willing-
ly lent his colt, albeit he had no knowledge of Jesus,
nor Jesus any right therein;—of the man bearing the
pitcher of water, who at once granted the upper chamber for the paschal supper;—of the multitudes whom
twice over he drove out of the temple, with all the
implements of their religious traffic, which zealous
invasion of their consecrated iniquities they would
with all their might have resisted; but they durst not,
so strong was the Holy Spirit in Jesus to strike them
all with consternation. And the same may we say of
the officers whom the Pharisees did send to take him,
but who returned saying, "Never man spake like this
man;" also of that rabble rout who came at midnight
to seize him, and were by the majesty of his words
stricken backwards to the ground. These two are instances—the one at the outset, the other at the termi-
nation of his public ministry—demonstrative of the
awful power which the Spirit can put forth from a
man, when it pleaseth him, enough to astound and lay
prostrate whole multitudes: and they further shew,
that Jesus ever possessed might enough to have over-
whelmed all his enemies, if he had not been withheld
by pity towards them, and ever impelled with the
strongest desire not to destroy but to save. This
power, I believe, still remaineth in the church, and
would be manifested to her faith, when necessary:
yea, and, I dare say, hath ofttimes been manifested
in behalf of persecuted saints, both in the way of
enabling them to escape out of the hands of their
enemies, and in the way of striking their enemies with
rnation. It is prophesied of the two witnesses,

that they shall have power to shut heaven in the days of their prophecy, and to afflict men with as many plagues as they please, and to bring fire down from heaven to consume their enemies. (Rev. xi.) Of this kind, also, is the power which was given to Jesus, by incredible presence and readiness of mind, to confound his adversaries, and with a single word to detect and scatter their cunning plots laid to entrap him in his words. Wisdom greater than the serpent's, with harmlessness as the dove's, is one of the attributes and functions of the Spirit with which he was anointed, and we by him.

Next to this, I place his power over diseases to heal them. That this belonged to him, not in virtue of his incommunicable Divinity, but of his anointed manhood, is manifest from the fact that he did convey it, along with the casting out of devils, to his Apostles and Disciples, when they went their rounds of preaching. And this work of the Spirit he commonly connected with the forgiveness of sins, which also he bequeathed to his church: " Whosesoever sins ye remit," &c. In this head I include all miracles done upon the body, in the way of healing, restoring, recovering, and even raising from the dead. They are all a form of the Holy Ghost's operation in the region of the superhuman and Divine : for it is proper to devils to afflict, to God only to cure. To the church this was solemnly bequeathed ; even to every one that believeth, and to the elders in particular. And, in point of fact, Peter and Paul both went as great lengths, if not greater than our Lord in this merciful ministry. And doubt is there none, that the church ought ever to have retained this token of an indwelling, merciful God.

Also, power superhuman over animated nature : as, for example, in the case of the wild beasts of the desert, with whom he sojourned during the forty days of the temptation—of the fish, which brought the tribute-money in his mouth to Peter's hook—of the two immense draughts which, at the will of Jesus, came at once into Peter's net—of the untamed colt

of an ass, whereon never man had rode, and which,
all wild and furious as in those countries it is, bore
him as meekly and gently as a lamb; also of the
sheep and the oxen which he drave out of the outer
court of the temple; not, as I think, by an act of
natural coercion, but by the power of the Spirit
going forth upon them, in earnest of that subjection
of sheep and oxen, fish, and creeping things which
is promised to him in the viiith Psalm. And,
finally, power over inanimate nature: as in the
instance of the water converted into wine—of the sea
made to upbear both him and Peter—of the stormy
winds turned into a calm—of the matter of bread
and fish multiplied manifold, in order to feed the
three thousand and the five thousand—of the fig-
tree cursed, and at once withered. All which—
with every other instance of superhuman power put
forth by Jesus in the days of his flesh, whereof only
a very small part indeed is recorded—are manifestations, not of the Divinity of the Son, but of the
Father in the Man by the Holy Spirit; manifestations of the power and virtue of the anointing of the
Holy Ghost which the Son of Man received at his
baptism in order to reveal him Son of God: first-fruits
of that power which was revealed in him in its full
strength, in the exceeding mightiness of its working,
at his resurrection; and which, all mighty as it is, the
Apostle declareth doth work in the same measure in
all who believe (Eph. i. 19); as Jesus also declared
that the believer should do as great, and greater works
than he did. But, by ascribing these works to the
Divinity of the Lord, instead of ascribing them to the
substance of the Holy Ghost, with which he was
anointed by the indwelling of the Father, it hath
come to be looked upon as little less than blasphemy
to hold that they should ever be done over again in
the members: whereby the work of the Holy Ghost
in the church is entirely defeated by false doctrine.
For this reason I have been at such pains to draw out
the Lord's ministry, and to exhibit it, not as a work
of the Second Person in his Godhead, but his work

in his manhood, through baptism with the Holy Ghost; and which is competent to be done in manhood always in virtue of the same baptism. In one word, I believe that, as Adam's life in its creation state is that work of the Holy Ghost with which every man is created—which sin hath marred, and redemption doth restore—so the life of Jesus, as exhibited after his baptism, is that work of the Holy Ghost of which every man at his baptism partaketh, according to his place and station in the body. For Christ is the Head, and we are but the members. We are not counterparts of Christ. He alone hath the fulness in himself; and the church, which is his body, hath that same fulness ever poured into herself : but we are only members in the body, having each a division or distribution proper to himself. Nevertheless, as the power in the Head is supernatural, so is the power in all and every one of the members of the like superhuman kind: and baptism with the Holy Ghost doth bring us into that superhuman sphere and region, to act the part therein which the great Lord and Master may deem to be most meet ; "the Spirit dividing to every one according to his will."

III. Having opened the prophetical testimony in the Old Testament upon the subject of the baptism with the Holy Ghost, and the example thereof in the actual life and ministry of our Lord, we now go into the record of his words to see what further light they cast upon the subject. Besides the last sermon to his disciples, which may be considered as the prophetical exposition of the whole matter, there are several briefer notices well worthy our attention, whereof the first is contained in the Sermon on the Mount, and is as follows :—

1. " Beware of false prophets, which come to you in sheep's clothing, but inwardly they are ravening wolves. Ye shall know them by their fruits. Do men gather grapes of thorns, or figs of thistles ? Even so every good tree bringeth forth good fruit; but a corrupt tree bringeth forth evil fruit. A good tree cannot bring forth evil fruit: neither can a corrupt

tree bring forth good fruit. Every tree that bringeth
not forth good fruit, is hewn down, and cast into the
fire. Wherefore by their fruits ye shall know them.
Not every one that saith unto me, Lord, Lord, shall
enter into the kingdom of heaven : but he that doeth
the will of my Father which is in heaven. Many
will say to me in that day, Lord, Lord, have we not
prophesied in thy name ? and in thy name have cast
out devils ? and in thy name done many wonderful
works ? And then will I profess unto them, I never
knew you : depart from me, ye that work iniquity"
(Matt. vii. 15—23). That *prophecy* holdeth of the
baptism with the Holy Ghost is beyond question both
from the prediction of Joel and the fulfilment thereof,
on the day of Pentecost ; and so also do the *casting
out of devils*, and the *working of many miracles;*
which are indeed the three great divisions of the
supernatural power—namely, power prophetical, to
utter things beyond the natural faculty, power over
unclean spirits, and power over the material world.
And all these Jesus declareth shall be found, at the
great day of revealing secrets, to have been possessed
by men whom he never knew, by workers of iniquity,
by ravening wolves in sheep's clothing. And these
not pretenders to the prophetic gift, but real pos-
sessors of it, who have actually had supernatural
powers of speech, exorcism, and miracle-working ;
and not only so, but who shall put them forth in the
name of Jesus. Now the question ariseth, Were these
possessed with false spirits which assumed Christ's
name ; or were they really possessed with supernatural powers from God, which they abused to their
own selfish and wicked purposes ? I believe both to
be possible, and to have actually existed in times
past, and as about to be revealed again, if not already revealed in the church. First, that there were
ministers of Satan who actually performed wonderful
works, calling themselves ministers of Christ in the
primitive times, is clear from those places of Scripture where the spirits are required to be proved, and
tests for that purpose are given (1 John iv. 1 ; 1 Cor.

xii. 3); and also from the following express declaration of the Apostle Paul: "For such are false
apostles, deceitful workers, transforming themselves
into the apostles of Christ. And no marvel; for
Satan himself is transformed into an angel of light.
Therefore it is no great thing if his ministers also be
transformed as the ministers of righteousness; whose
end shall be according to their works" (2 Cor. xi.
13—15). And that the like shall occur again, nigh
unto the time of the Lord's appearing, is by himself
predicted in these words: "For there shall arise
false Christs and false prophets, and shall shew great
signs and wonders, insomuch that (if it were possible) they shall deceive the very elect" (Matt. xxiv.
24). And if I am not greatly misinformed, these
unclean spirits may be found in full operation under
the disguise of Christian truth and sanctity among
the followers of Joanna Southcote in this very land.
Oh, how I tremble for the present unprepared state
of the church, so uninstructed in things supernatural, so taught to surrender its faith upon the shew
of things miraculous. The doctrine which is constantly taught in the schools, " Shew me a miracle, and
I must reason or think no more, but only listen and
believe," hath prepared the church for Satan's workings whenever it pleaseth him to appear. The more
need that men do instantly betake themselves from
all such doctors to the great Teacher, who giveth, as
the only test for trying persons supernaturally gifted,
to know their fruits, that is, their good words and
works—a test which requireth our own conscience to
be clear and our own life to be sanctified by the continual indwelling of the Spirit of love and truth.
Without whom I believe it is not possible to discern
between the workings of an unclean and a clean
spirit in the men whom they have possessed. Oh,
how merciful is Jesus to his church in restraining
those evil spirits from coming forth ! and when the
time is come for loosing them, he will shew his power
over them in his elect. But this is not all, I further
believe that the Lord in the passage before us refers,

and that principally, to persons who, having received the gifts supernatural, did use them for partial and private ends, to the detriment of the church and the shipwreck of their own souls. That this is possible, is manifest from the history of the Corinthian church, whose zeal for spirits and spiritual things betrayed them into all manner of carnality, and brought the church to the very edge of dissolution. These gifts not being employed for the ends of charity and edification, were the occasion of much sin, yea and even enormities, to correct which the First Epistle to that church was written. That one might fall away, after having received the fullest distribution of superhuman power, is further manifested from what is written; " For it is impossible for those who were once enlightened, and have tasted of the heavenly gift, and were made partakers of the Holy Ghost, and have tasted the good word of God, and the powers of the world to come, if they shall fall away, to renew them again unto repentance; seeing they [while they] crucify to themselves the Son of God afresh, and put him to an open shame " (Heb. vi. 4—6). Persons baptized with the Holy Ghost might apostatize, and, apostatizing, did carry out along with them the gifts with which they had been endowed, serving themselves and Satan therewith. And however fearful this consideration may be, I believe it to be the very case contemplated by our Lord in the passage under consideration ; because they are said to cast out devils, which Beelzebub would not do. For when the Pharisees alleged this against the miracles of Jesus, his answer implied as much as, that Beelzebub would not cast out Beelzebub.—As however the full consideration of this case will come before us in our next quotation, we postpone it here, and observe further upon the passage at present before us, that neither prophecy not casting out of devils, nor doing of wonderful works, in the name of Jesus, is any certain proof and demonstration of being in a saved state ; nay, nor even of ever having known Jesus, or having done the will of his Father in heaven.

This is very mysterious, and at first sight unaccount-
able; but our part is, to learn from the word a right
notion of the baptism with the Holy Ghost, and
not to impose our preconceived notions upon the
infallible word. It would seem then, that as hypo-
critical persons might receive the sacrament of baptism, so also might they be made partakers of the
Holy Ghost, and abuse it to their own selfish and
wicked ends; for unless the mind of Jesus be in us,
and we be informed with his life, we will always
serve the ends of the fallen creature, and not the
ends of God. For one, therefore, who is not conscious to himself of being grafted into Christ, to
pray for the gifts of the Spirit, is verily to seek more
means of dishonouring the Lord our God. It would
seem that the gifts of the Spirit were intended to go
along with baptism in the ministrations of the church;
and that indiscriminately, as was the case in the
church of Samaria (Acts viii.); in the company of
Cornelius (Acts x.); and in the church of Ephesus,
(Acts xix.); and I well believe also, with those baptized on the day of Pentecost, though it be not mentioned as a fact, but only declared as a promise.
Now as it may well be feared, that, if there was a
Judas amongst the twelve, there would be some hy-
pocrites and backsliders amongst those churches, it
would necessarily happen, that the gifts of the Spirit
would extend beyond the number of the elect of
God, and true members of Jesus Christ. For the
gifts and calling of God are without repentance;
being given, they are given, and not revoked, and
the responsibility of them resteth evermore with those
who have received them. This important doctrine
was taught in the example of Judas, who had, no
doubt, as full an endowment of miraculous powers
as the rest of the Apostles, though he was a thief
and betrayed his Master. Truly it doth mightily
increase the guilt of a man to be introduced into this
region of superhuman power of Divine inworking,
and still to resist and rebel against God. But yet it
is possible in order to shew, that of that region also

Christ is the only Lord, and that spiritual persons are dependent for their salvation as entirely upon Jesus as they were before they received their spiritual baptism. Solemnly therefore do I counsel those who have not been baptized with the Holy Ghost, to seek first the indwelling of Jesus, that they may abide in him, and that his words may abide in them, before they seek the indwelling of the Father. Most solemnly also do I counsel those who have received power from on high, to be only the more jealous over their allegiance and obedience unto Jesus: for though God in that region is the same gracious God as in every other, yet there also will he suffer no name to be exalted but the name of Jesus; and no will to be done but his, who is the Lord of all.

2. The next notice of this subject, contained in the Gospels, is to be found in the xiith chapter of Matthew, from the 22d to the 38th verse. It originated in Christ's having healed one possessed with a devil, blind and dumb; which act of spiritual supremacy the Pharisees ascribed to Beelzebub, saying, " This fellow doth not cast out devils, but by Beelzebub the prince of the devils." Whereunto Jesus gave a twofold reply; the first in these words : " Every kingdom divided against itself is brought to desolation; and every city or house divided against itself shall not stand : and if Satan cast out Satan, he is divided against himself; how shall then his kingdom stand?" (vers. 25, 26.) This seems to me as much as to say, that Satan would not give power to be used against himself in casting devils out; and therefore if we see any one do this thing, it is a sign that he is possessed with superhuman power of God's bestowing, and not of Satan's : and accordingly we find this enumerated first amongst the signs which follow them that believe. " In my name shall they cast out devils" (Mark xvi. 17). He next maketh answer to their envious and wicked insinuations by removing the question from himself unto their children : " And if I by Beelzebub cast out devils, by whom do your children cast them out? therefore they

shall be your judges" (Matt. xii. 27). By this appeal
it is manifest, that in those days the casting out of
devils in the name of Jesus, was a thing practised,
not only by the Twelve and the Seventy (Luke x. 17),
but likewise by others, who haply, seeing the power of
that name in these commissioned men, conceived faith,
and, without waiting instructions from Jesus, went
forth straightway, and proceeded in faith and benevolence to the work of casting devils out. Whereof one
instance is recorded to us (Mark ix. 38, 39); which
Jesus would not put a stop to, because the man was
doing it out of a good intention, saying, " Forbid him
not : for there is no man which shall do a miracle in
my name, that can lightly speak evil of me. For
he that is not against us is on our part" (vers. 39,
40). But when certain of the vagabond Jews, ex-
orcists, took upon them to call over them which had
evil spirits the name of the Lord Jesus, they prevailed
not ; but the spirit did prevail against them, because
they were not believers in that name which they
named, but did make use of it for gain. This adds
another lesson to what we have learned already ; to
wit, that though God will dispense this heavenly
baptism to persons who are not elect but fall away,
he doth not and will not bestow it upon any one who
speaketh lightly of Jesus, or embraceth the faith of
Jesus out of a sinister intention. The gift is not
bestowed save upon those who are well minded
towards Jesus, yet doth not prove him who receiveth
it to be of the election of the Father, which is essentially hid with the Father; nor doth secure him against
falling away, which is not otherwise prevented than
by abiding in Jesus ; while, at the same time, it ad-
vanceth him into a new region both of knowledge and
of power, with new privileges and new responsibilities
attendant thereon.

Jesus, having thus, by direct teaching of truth,
and by an appeal from their envy of him to their natural love of their children, sought to deliver them
from their blasphemy of the Holy Ghost in his acts
manifested, doth not rest there, but proceedeth to

graft upon the incident most important instruction
and warning. The instruction is contained in these
words: " If I cast out devils by the Spirit of God,
then the kingdom of God is come unto you. Or else
how can one enter into a strong man's house, and
spoil his goods, except he first bind the strong man?
and then he will spoil his house. He that is not with
me is against me; and he that gathereth not with
me scattereth abroad" (Matt. xii. 28—30). These
words declare, that the casting out of devils is an infallible proof of the power of God triumphing over
the power of Satan; so that wherever we see this
proceeding, we may be sure the kingdom of God is
there, and we ought to join ourselves thereto. We
ought to stand in awe at such signs and tokens, and
not blaspheme them ; because therein we would be
blaspheming the mighty power of God, and bringing upon our head the most direful judgment, written
in these words immediately following: " Wherefore
I say unto you, All manner of sin and blasphemy
shall be forgiven unto men: but the blasphemy against
the Holy Ghost shall not be forgiven unto men. And
whosoever speaketh a word against the Son of Man,
it shall be forgiven him: but whosoever speaketh
against the Holy Ghost, it shall not be forgiven him,
neither in this world, neither in the world to come"
(vers. 31, 32). These words are of too fearful a nature to be left in a loose and indefinite condition, and
therefore I feel it my duty to protest against their
being applied to any other case than that for which
they were evidently written; to wit, the case of men
ascribing unto evil agency the manifestations of the
Holy Ghost. To speak a word against the Son of
Man, is to doubt or deny, and even to contemn and
upbraid, the doctrine, that Jesus of Nazareth, the
Son of Man, is God manifest in the flesh: and this
can be forgiven ; because He is God manifested in
weakness, humiliation, mortality, and misery: but
for a man to blaspheme the Holy Ghost, manifested
in casting out devils and otherwise, is to speak against
God manifested in the full blaze of his power and

goodness and grace. And seeing there is no higher
nor fuller exhibition of him to be made, deliberately to
reject this and to call it of the devil or of some other
evil origin, is to put away from us the perfection of
Divine beauty and goodness and power, and to debar
ourselves from ever entering into the inheritance of
his blessedness. It is manifest from what follows
this most fearful utterance of the Lord, that he had
respect therein to *words* spoken against the Holy
Ghost; for he straightway proceedeth to shew men,
that as the character of the fruit depended on the
character of the tree, so our words depend upon our
hearts, and that such blasphemous words did bespeak
an evil and corrupt heart: wherefore he would have
them know that by our words we shall be justified,
and by our words we shall be condemned in the day
of judgment. My heart is exceeding heavy while I
indite these things; for I feel assured that the time
is near when the church in these lands shall be
brought to this perilous test. We shall ere long
have lifted up amongst us the full manifestation of the
Holy Ghost, which is already present in the speaking
with tongues; and when to this are added the other
manifestations (and the time, I believe, is not distant),
then things are come to a crisis with the church;
and she must either decide for the Holy Ghost or
against him, for her own salvation or her own perdition for ever and ever. It is the sense of this near
and unknown crisis which chiefly moveth me to put
forth these views of the baptism of the Holy Ghost;
that, by the grace and mercy of God, I may do my
part to prevent the overhanging ruin, and lead many,
if not all, away from the brink of perdition unto the
green pastures and still waters of peace and truth
and love.

3. The next promise concerneth the liberty which we
have in asking, the delight which God hath in giving,
the Holy Ghost. It is contained in the xi th chapter of Luke, and arose out of a request on the part of
our Lord's disciples that he would teach them to pray ;
whereupon he gave them that form of words com-

L

monly called the Lord's Prayer: and the more to encourage them in the office of prayer, "that they might always pray and not faint," he added a parable, to exhibit the power of importunity to prevail over the most unpromising and hopeless circumstances. As if he had foreseen the present low estate of the church, without any bread in the house even for her own children, he supposeth the case of a man upon whom a friend comes in unexpectedly from a long journey at midnight, when he has not a morsel to set before him. Can this be the nobleman who went a far journey, and comes home at the dead of night, when the virgins all slumbered and slept? Be this as it may, the case is exactly in point for us, at this present time, visited all of a sudden with the tidings of Christ's instant return, and having no oil for our lamps, nor comely raiment to appear with in his sight. At such a moment, when we are all but utterly destitute of the Holy Ghost, it was a most provident and gracious act of our Lord's, to put forth the liberty of asking and receiving that gift which maketh the King's daughter all glorious within, and covereth her outwardly with raiment of needlework, under this semblance of an unprovided man hasting out at midnight for loaves wherewith to appease the hunger of his weary and wayworn friend. And, as if to silence all doubt and cavil, he puts it so that the friend to whom he addressed himself should be in bed with his children, and give a flat and peremptory refusal to the petition : "Trouble me not ; the door is now shut, and my children are with me in bed ; I cannot rise and give thee." This signifies that the Father, whose office it is to give the Holy Ghost, may not bestow so soon as asked, may have retired within the curtains of silence, and for a long time closed the door of communication with mortals, as indeed hath long been felt by the church. But, even in such a case, importunity will certainly prevail over this and every obstacle whatever. For hear with what words of glorious assurance the Lord concludes this parable, so appropriate to our present desolation: "I say unto you, Though he will not rise and give him because he is his friend, yet because of his importunity he will rise and give him as many as he needeth. And I say unto you, Ask, and it shall be given you; seek, and ye shall find; knock, and it shall be opened unto you. For every one that asketh, receiveth; and he that seeketh, findeth; and to him that knocketh, it shall be opened. If a son shall ask bread of any of you that is a father, will he give him a stone? or if he ask a fish, will he for a fish give him a serpent? or if he shall ask an egg, will he offer him a scorpion? If ye then, being evil, know how to give good gifts unto your children, how much more shall your heavenly Father give the Holy Spirit to them that ask him?" (Luke xi. 8—13.)

Many a time, before I knew the great end of this promise as I now do know it, have I held it up to the admiration of the church as the most beautiful, most perfect, and most blessed of all those varied utterances whereby God hath sought to make assurance of his love and goodness doubly sure to his doubting and erring children. The threefold form of entreaty, "ask, seek, knock," rising in importunity the one above the other; together with the corresponding forms of assurance, "ye shall receive, ye shall find, it shall be opened to you," varied in expression for the end of confirming our faith; next, the repetition of the whole in a new style of absolute and positive assertion; then, the introduction of the three strongest impossibilities which can be conceived amongst men; and, finally, the multiplying of that impossibility manifold by appealing to the perfect goodness and holiness of God;—these wonderful combinations of thought and language, do, when taken together, express the most powerful encouragement and intense assurance which it is possible to conceive. And what is the object of such solicitous and laboured encouragement? Is it some cheap and common benefit, like the light of the sun or the fertilizing rain on the fruitful earth? or is it the common benefit of God's mercy and grace, which we sinners enjoy in the holy life and death of Jesus in this our sinful flesh? or is it the gift of faith and of salvation from the wrath to come, which is proper to all the elect? No; but it is the Holy Ghost in his largest and fullest operation, in all his power and efficacy, in all his gifts and graces, which is thus liberally offered and undoubtingly assured to every one who with sincerity asketh, with earnestness seeketh, and with importunity knocketh. And after such a manifold asseveration from the mouth of Him who is the Truth, we surely will not dare to assign our want or shortcoming in the powers and gifts of the Holy Ghost to any cause but one only; our own remissness in asking, or, if we have seemed to ask much, to our asking without the faith that we should receive what we asked for. All doubt on this head to remove from the minds of his disciples, to assure us that God felt no reluctance to bestow the Holy Ghost,—but, contrariwise, that it is more unnatural for him to refuse our prayers for the same than for a father to withhold bread and other nourishments from his craving children, to the end we might pray without the shadow of a doubt,—our Lord hath built up this wonderful argument.

But there is a still stronger point in our Lord's discourse, to which the ungodliness and uncharitableness of this age obligeth me to make reference; which is, that when we ask for "good gifts," God will not give us evil and hurtful things in answer to our prayers. For I have heard it asserted, and that not by scoffers but by apparently very spiritual persons, that it was a perilous thing to ask for those gifts of the Holy Spirit which are not now in the church, lest we should obtain what we sought, and find that we had got what might prove a temptation and even an injury to us. And others, who are praying constantly for the Holy Ghost, do look upon those gifts which have appeared amongst the brethren, as works of delusion or effects of excitement. They allow the people in whom they have shewed

themselves to be a godly people, and their prayers
to be sincere prayers; but that which they have received and do manifest, they hold to be an evil thing
by all means to be discountenanced and discouraged.
They allow that they have asked for bread, but they
say that they have received a stone; instead of a fish,
a serpent; and instead of an egg, a scorpion. But
how can this be, if God be, as our Lord describeth him
in this passage, infinitely more considerate and tender
than a father to his children? who, if they were to ask
any thing which would be hurtful to them, would be as
careful to withhold, as he would be delighted to grant
whatever was good. And, as if to put this question
to rest, the Holy Ghost, in the parallel passage, hath
directed the Evangelist Matthew to use this very
word " good things :" " How much more shall your
Father which is in heaven give good things to them
that ask him?" It is utterly an erroneous and a
most unworthy notion of God, that if we ask any
thing to our disprofit, we must nevertheless and surely shall receive it. No: He knoweth our weakness,
and kindly considereth and provideth against it. He
will not put into our hands a weapon for harming us.
Every thing which we receive from him is not only
in itself good, but good for us to receive; a precious
talent which we may indeed abuse, but which we
ought to trade with and improve for the Giver's sake,
and for our own future reward in the day of reckon-
ing. Let no one be afraid, therefore, to ask good
things from God, from whom cometh down every
good and perfect gift; and least of all let him be
afraid to ask for the Holy Ghost, who is the complete
procession of all good from Him who is the Good One.
And this is the reason why in the one case the word
" goods," and in the other the word " Holy Ghost,"
is used ; because all goods that the Father hath are
given to Christ, and by him sent to us under the
hand of the Holy Ghost. The Holy Ghost which
proceedeth from the Father and the Son, bringeth
with him the effluence of their goodness. I can conceive indeed, and even believe, that God will punish

the wicked, and perhaps chastise his own children when they grieve him, by granting them quails to please their flesh, while he sendeth leanness into their souls. And if any one be seeking gifts for the mere pride and power and notoriety of possessing them, I entreat them to desist, lest they receive that which will be sure to prove in their hands for a bane and a curse: but if any one for the prosperity of their own souls in holiness, for the edification of the church in unity, and for the manifestation of the power of the Father, Son, and Holy Ghost, shall pray for such a distribution of the Holy Ghost as may seem to the great Lord most meet to their place in the body, it shall not on any wise be refused. And he need not be afraid that God will send in its stead an evil fruit of enthusiasm, fanaticism, or diabolical delusion. But let him keep his heart and mind in Christ Jesus, otherwise he will wander into some form of error, and use his gift for some end of evil. That which he received as a true gift of the Spirit, may become an instrument of the flesh, and end in the most abominable and foul prostitution of the Spirit to sensuality. This ariseth from forgetting our responsibility to Christ, and yielding ourselves to the gift, or else using it for other ends than the edification of the whole body.

The MAN Jesus is the Lord of the Spirit, and the mystery of godliness standeth in this, that the Holy Ghost hath condescended to act under the direction of man, as the Son of God hath humbled himself to become man, and God hath purposed to be bodied forth in the form of man. As it is with the Head, so with the members upholden by the Head. They also are expected under Christ to rule in the gift, and not by the gift to be overruled ; and if from this personal responsibility they turn away, then do I perceive that the flesh and the gift may intermingle in frightful and hideous confusion. For what keeps down the flesh but our personal will sustained by Christ the Head ? and if we, upon receiving a spiritual gift, do yield our will thereto, then is the

flesh relieved from his master, and cometh in with
all his natural violence to mingle in every thing which
we utter. With those who abandon themselves to
the gift, instead of regulating its use by the laws
and commandments of Jesus for the ends of love
and goodness, the gift will prove hurtful and not
profitable to the personal sanctification and the edification of the church. Their utterances may become
worse than profitless, scandals and stumbling-blocks
to the spiritual; to the carnal, occasions of mockery
and blasphemy. And therefore it is an essential
element of all this doctrine, that "the spirits of the
prophets are subject to the prophets." Therefore
also it is that the gift cometh in the form of persons, "apostles, evangelists, prophets, pastors and
teachers," and not in the form of things.

This therefore is the truth, that if a man be sincere with God, and ask of him out of a sense of his
wants, he may ask all things which the Holy Ghost
hath proceeded from the Father into the Son to bear
unto the needy creatures of God. When I can find
any declaration in Scripture to the effect that the
gifts are not manifestations of the Holy Ghost, and
that it is not the same Holy Ghost which worketh
them who worketh the graces and the fruits also, then
I shall give heed to suspicions and surmises upon the
liberty of asking for the gifts, equally with the fruits
and graces: but finding Holy Scripture doth give all
these equally and alike to the one and the same Spirit,
I will regard all such suspicions and surmises as the
fruits of that spirit "which now worketh in the
children of disobedience;" whose main effort it is
in all ways to "quench the Holy Ghost," and to
"despise prophesyings." With respect to their
timorous precautions, as if there were some more
danger in asking one operation of the Holy Ghost than
in asking another, there is not the shadow of a foundation for any such feelings. The Holy Ghost is not
divided, nor can his operations be separated. He
who asks for Him doth not surely prescribe to
Him his mode of operating, but leaves that unto the

Father and the Son, from whom he proceedeth, and
to the Spirit who divideth unto every man according
to his will. Nor is it right to say, that we must wait
for perfect sanctification before we ask for the manifestations of the Spirit, which are given to every man
to profit withal, to edify oneself, and to edify the
church. In the Epistles, which contain the authentic
records of spiritual gifts, they went along with the
preaching of the Gospel, to confirm it to the believer
(1 Cor. i. 6; Eph. i. 13), and with baptism as a part
of the inward and spiritual grace thereof (Acts ii. 38),
and were thus early given in order to constitute the
membership and organization of a church, through
the use of which the church might grow up into perfection, " making increase of itself in love." So
far from being extraordinary gifts proper to a mature
state of the church, they are like the members and
organs of the child, the instruments by which it is
to grow up unto its estate of maturity (1 Cor. xii.;
Eph. iv). All such objections therefore are but in-
ventions of Satan, and those whom he hath beguiled
into his service, to bar the way of our freedom to
God, and to damp the ardour of the church after
her own perfection. And I do bless our Lord and
Saviour, that, when opening our liberty to apply for
the Holy Ghost, he did it in such language as neither
the ingenuity of the sophist, nor the profanity of the
blasphemer can turn aside. " If ye then being evil,
know how to give good gifts unto your children, how
much more shall your heavenly Father give the Holy
Ghost to them that ask him ? " I need no other warrant to ask for the Holy Ghost in all his functions.
He that doth is an unbeliever ; and, by God's grace,
I will not cease to pray, and to teach, and to believe,
till he make the church of which I am pastor to come
behind in no gift, waiting for the coming of the Lord
Jesus Christ. And I do beseech every faithful and
enlightened minister to persevere in the same course;
and exhort the people, whose ministers oppose this
work, to meet and pray for the increase and edification of the churches to which they belong.

P3/+

Printed in the United States
111126LV00008B/115/A